ALLIED FIGHTERS OF WORLD WAR TWO: US AND BRITAIN

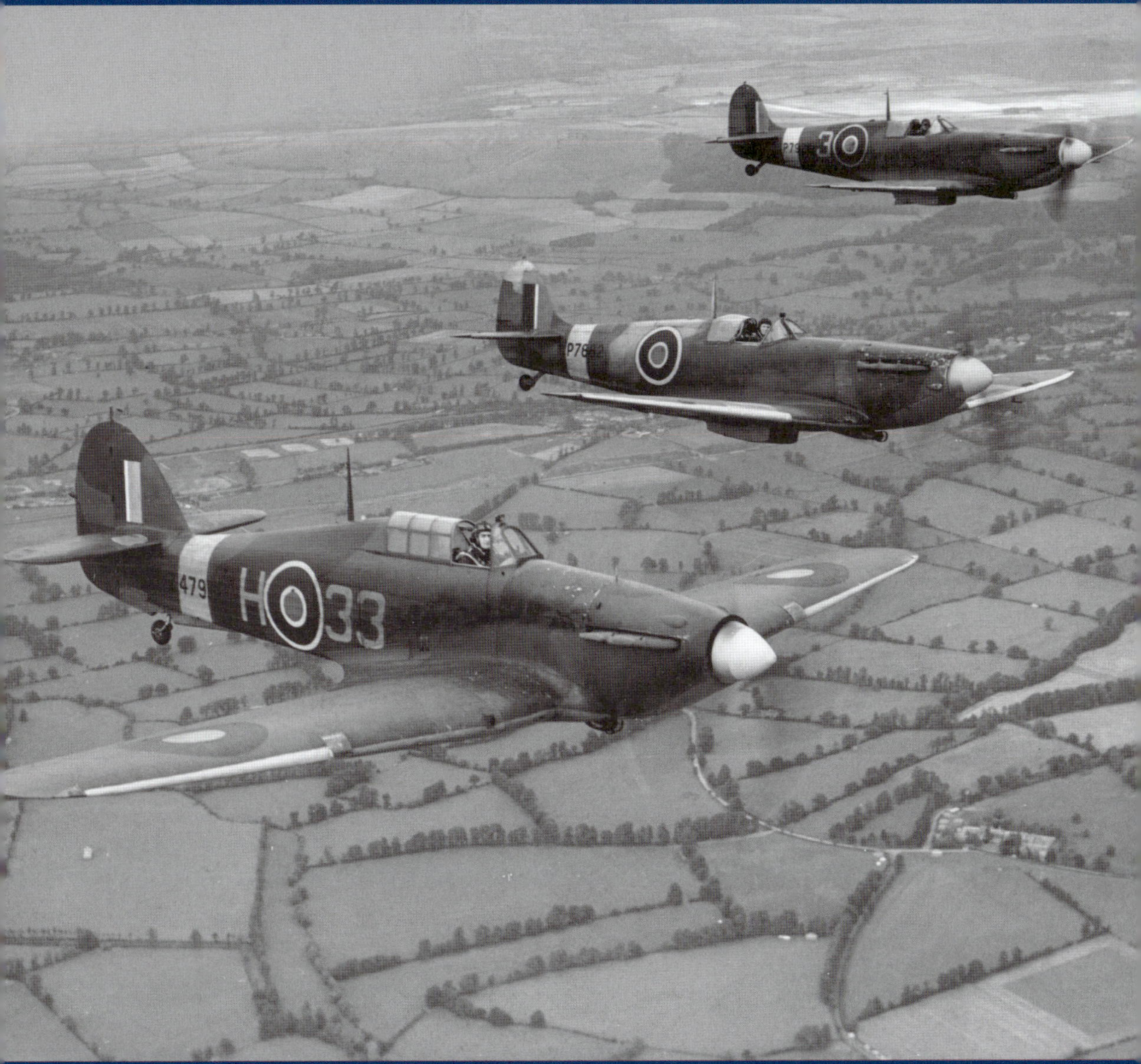

Published by Key Books

An imprint of Key Publishing Ltd, PO Box 100, Stamford, Lincs, PE9 1XQ

www.keypublishing.com

Original editions published as *Aeroplane Collectors' Archive: British Fighters of World War 2* © 2012, edited by Mike Hooks
and as *Aeroplane Special Aviation Archive: US Fighters of World War II* © 2014, edited by Martyn Chorlton

This edition © 2023

All images: Key Archive, unless noted. Designed by Panda Media

ISBN 978 1 80282 584 8

All rights reserved. Reproduction in whole or in part in any form whatsoever or by any means is strictly prohibited without the prior permission of the Publisher.

CONTENTS

4	Introduction	110	XP-51, P-51, P-51A and Mustang II
6	Bell P-39 Airacobra	112	P-51B, P-51C and Mustang III
8	P-61 Black Widow	118	P-51D, K and Mustang IV
14	Bristol Beaufighter	126	Supermarine Spitfire
30	Curtiss P-36 and Hawk 75 Family	138	Hawker Tempest
36	Boulton Paul Defiant	142	Republic P-47B and C Thunderbolt
46	Gloster Gladiator	146	Republic P-47D Thunderbolt
56	Hawker Hurricane	152	Curtiss P-40, A to C/Tomahawk Mk I, IIA and IIB
72	A-36A Apache (AKA Invader)	156	Hawker Typhoon
78	Lockheed P-38 Lightning	162	Westland Whirlwind
84	Curtiss P-40D to Q Warhawk/Kittyhawk I, IA, II, II and IV	168	Waiting in the Wings – British
90	Gloster Meteor	172	Waiting in the Wings – US
98	De Havilland Mosquito		

Introduction

These two aircraft from the RAF's Battle of Britain Memorial Flight illustrate one of the oldest Spitfire survivors, P7350, and also the last Hurricane built, PZ865.

THINK FIGHTER, THINK GLAMOUR

It is true now and it was true then – almost every aspiring military pilot wants to fly fighters. This was particularly true in World War Two, the era when the fighter aircraft really came of age and the names passed into legend: Spitfire, Hurricane, Mustang, Thunderbolt.

Why did fighters have such appeal? They were fast, certainly. They grabbed a lot of headlines. They were easy on the eye, too. Fighters looked better than any aircraft before them and to this day, World War Two fighters still look as beautiful as anything produced by post-war or current and emerging technologies. At almost any airshow display, it is the World War Two fighters that are the tear jerkers.

Perhaps it is because fighters recall the myth of knightly chivalry, of single combat. Flown by a single pilot, armed with a battery of machine guns and/or cannon (and later on, bombs and rockets), the fighter very often offered a simple choice – kill or be killed by another single opponent either more skilled, experienced or just plain luckier. Of course, the truth was much more complicated.

If you successfully qualified as a fighter pilot – and, crucially, survived long enough – the opportunities to fly a wide mix of fast-changing aircraft and variants, designed and built to overcome the enormous demands of the greatest conflict the world has ever seen, were many.

This book focuses on the fighter aircraft of Britain and the United States during the war. That does not mean American dominance and a British supporting role – this was a period when British design innovation, skills and execution played an extraordinary and vital role in the path to victory.

While eager to avoid war, by the second half of the 1930s, the British government recognised the Nazi threat and escalated both design and manufacturing programmes in aviation. That decisions bore fruit when Britain stood alone in 1940 and 1941. The British-designed and -built cutting-edge technologies of the Hawker Hurricane and Supermarine Spitfire, powered by mighty Rolls-Royce engines, were instrumental in halting the previously invincible German war machine during the Battle of Britain.

It is a fact often forgotten that British aviation design and engineering excellence in fighters did not stop at the Battle of Britain. Hawker's Typhoon and Tempest, the Bristol Beaufighter and the de Havilland Mosquito (the 'Wooden Wonder') all more than earned their place in the aviation pantheon, showing astonishing versatility in the process. Their stories are fascinating, as are those of their less well-known counterparts that were developed, but for varying reasons, never made it into active service.

Across the pond, there was no shortage of recruits to the United States Army Air Corps (USAAC) following the US's abrupt entry into the war following the attack on Pearl Harbor on 7 December 1941.

Unlike the British, the USAAC was not given an opportunity to build up its forces and the developmental race was slow to start for American aircraft manufacturers. Most were more occupied with supplying to European air forces, with proposals for new aircraft designs stemming from either British or French sources. Curtiss, in particular, supplied large numbers of Hawks to France before that country's fall in June 1940 and Bell was despatching its P-39 to the Soviets many months before the US entered the war.

However, the USAAC (USAAF from 20 June 1941) was not entirely unprepared for war and the Curtiss production lines were already tooled up for mass P-40 production, which would continue much longer than expected, considering that the aircraft was not at the cutting edge of technology. Regardless, the P-40 became one of the big four American fighters of World War Two, the other three being the P-38 Lightning, P-47 Thunderbolt and the P-51 Mustang.

The pressures of war very rarely produce non-conformist aircraft, and even if they do, their chances of reaching production are slim; however, this philosophy was shattered with the P-38 Lightning. More than 10,000 were built to serve as the primary USAAF long-range escort fighter before the arrival of the P-47, which, in turn, found itself in a ground attack role while the P-51 took on the task during the latter stages of the war.

Like the British, the American fighter story is one of design innovation and engineering brilliance. More than 55,000 P-38s, P-40s, P-47s and P-51s were built between 1939 and 1946; more than enough to fight the Germans in North Africa, the Mediterranean and Europe and the Japanese in the Far East and the Pacific.

Allied Fighters of World War Two: US and Britain is about great airframes and great engineering combined with bold vision and execution.

Pilots of the 83rd Fighter Squadron (FS), 78th Fighter Group (FG) at Duxford in July 1944. The group served at Duxford, designated as USAAF Station 357, from April 1943 until October 1945.

BELL P-39 AIRACOBRA

Designed by R. J. Woods and O. L. Woodson, the Bell P-39 Airacobra broke new ground in fighter development, especially with regard to improving forward fire power. This resulted in an unusual arrangement where the fighter's Allison engine was mounted within the fuselage, behind the cockpit. As a result, the propeller was driven by a long shaft that travelled below the pilot's seat and on to a reduction gearbox in the nose of the aircraft. Forward armament included a 37mm cannon that fired through the propeller hub, a pair of .5in machine guns mounted in the upper forward fuselage and up to four .303in machine guns mounted in the wings, which combined gave the P-39 quite a clout. It was the decision to mount such a substantial cannon in the nose that dictated the position of the engine; a design problem that was overcome from the start in the Messerschmitt Bf 109. Thanks to the space created in the nose because of the engine position, the P-39 was fitted with a tricycle undercarriage; thus making the P-39 the first single-seat fighter with such a configuration to enter US Army service.

The prototype, XP-39, was first flown on 6 April 1938, and on 10 August 1939, the fighter was ordered into production. Following several pre-production aircraft, the first order for 80 machines was made up of 20 P-39Cs and 60 P-39Ds, the latter featuring self-sealing fuel tanks and the capability to carry a single 500lb or 75-US gallon drop tank. The P-39D was the first of many variants that was delivered to the USAAC from April 1941 onwards. The first export order was placed by Britain for 675 aircraft, originally named 'Caribou' but later changed to Airacobra. The first Airacobras arrived in Britain in July 1941 and, in September, 601 Squadron was re-equipped with the type. The RAF was disappointed with the aircraft, which was only destined to fly one operation before being withdrawn. Only 36 Airacobras (22 with 601 Squadron) are credited with serving in the RAF, the remainder of the order had been diverted to Russia (200) and the USAAF by late 1942. All ex-British Airacobras in the USAAF had the designation P-400.

In total, 9,584 P-39s were built, the most prolific variant being the P-39Q, of which 4,719 were supplied to Russia alone. In Soviet hands, half of the top ten fighter aces achieved their tally with the P-39, which remained in service with the 16th Guards Fighter Aviation Division until 1949.

In USAAF service, the P-39 saw action across the Pacific and in the Mediterranean Theatre of Operation (MTO), the type proving to be most useful at low level where it was effective at carrying out strafing and bombing attacks. Due to a lack of a turbocharger, the aircraft was a poor performer at altitude, which was one of several reasons why the RAF rejected it. However, there was always a role in the USAAF for the type to play and the P-39 more than held its ground against the Japanese at low level with the 5th and 13th Air Forces. In the MTO, the type was not introduced until early 1944 with the 99th Fighter Squadron (FS), and the 81st and 350th Fighter Groups (FGs). By mid-1944, the P-39 had been withdrawn from operations, its position taken over by the P-47 Thunderbolt.

Some of the 9,584 P-39s built, awaiting flight testing and delivery to Russia at Bell's Wheatfield, Buffalo factory. In total 4,719 P-39s were delivered to Russia, the bulk of them via Iran, between 1941 and 1945.

BELL P-39Q AIRACOBRA
FIRST FLIGHT: (YP-39) 6 April 1938
ENGINE: One 1,200hp Allison V-1710-85
WINGSPAN: 34ft
LENGTH: 30ft 2in
MAX SPEED: 376mph
CLIMB RATE: 3,750ft/min
ARMAMENT: One 37mm M4 cannon; two .5in Browning M2 and four .303in Browning M1919 machine guns

P-61 BLACK WIDOW

Up to the arrival of the P-61 Black Widow in 1944, all fighters operating in the night fighter role had not been specifically modified for this task. This made the P-61 unique because, from the first line drawn, this aircraft was designed from the outset for fighting at night.

As big as a medium bomber and with a crew of three made up of a pilot, air gunner and radar operator, the P-61 had its roots in a British, rather than an American, requirement. Back in 1940, the British were at full stretch with regard to applying further resources into the design and development of a new night fighter. Instead, Northrop was approached with the British specification, which called for a heavily-armed night fighter, with radar and endurance long enough to stay up all night if necessary. However, before negotiations had progressed, the USAAF produced its own set of specifications that generally matched the British idea and, as a result, the P-61 was developed.

The prototype XP-61 made its maiden flight on 26 May 1942, and instantly made quite an impression. The big fighter featured many innovations, including spoiler-type ailerons which enabled for the fitment of near full-span flaps and had the knock-on effect of expanding the aircraft's speed range and meant, despite its size, that the P-61 could operate from small airfields.

Deliveries of the P-61A began in October 1943 and, despite its daunting appearance, the aircraft was an instant hit with its pilots because of its excellent manoeuvrability. All extreme manoeuvres could be carried out with ease including a loop, barrel roll or Immelman turn. The P-61 could even be slow rolled on one engine with the manoeuvre being carried out into the dead engine, which would normally be fatal, and still is for many twin-engined aircraft. A good turner at all speeds down to 90mph, the P-61's stall was also benign in all configurations and at no point would drop a wing and plunge earth-bound out of control.

It was the 422nd Night Fighter Squadron (NFS) that finally received its first P-61As at Scorton in June 1944 after a few months of wrangling between senior officers who declared that the Black Widow was not up to the job and that the Mosquito should be used instead. The first kill over Europe for the P-61 was a V-1 flying bomb, shot down by Lt Herman Ernst on 16 July 1944. In the Pacific theatre, it was the 6th NFS on Guadalcanal that received its first P-61s in June 1944 in place of the P-70. The first operation was flown on 25 June, and five days later, the unit's first kill, a G4M 'Betty', was shot down.

The P-61A was succeeded by the P-61B, which featured pylons for drops tanks or bombs and a dorsal turret with four 0.5in machine guns, which was missing from the majority of P-61As. The final production P-61C featured turbocharged engines but only 41 had been delivered when production came to an end in August 1945, a total of 706 Black Widows having been built. Redesignated as the F-61 in USAF service, the Black Widow was not retired until 1950, by which time the jet age had firmly taken over.

Two of the three crew of this P-61A pose for the camera, which can be dated to no earlier than June 1944 thanks to the half-invasion strikes under each boom. Appropriately named, the Black Widow was a sinister looking machine from any angle.

P-61 Black Widow

Northrop P-61A-1-NO Black Widow 42-5526 *Nightie Mission* of the 6th NFS taking on 646 US-gallons AN-F-48 100/130 octane fuel at Guadalcanal in August 1944. This aircraft survived but was condemned for salvage on 31 August 1945.

P-61B-1-NO BLACK WIDOW
FIRST FLIGHT: (XP-61) 26 May 1942
ENGINES: Two 2,000hp Pratt & Whitney R-2800-65 Double Wasp 18-cylinder radial
WINGSPAN: 66ft ¾in
LENGTH: 49ft 7in
HEIGHT: 14ft 8in
EMPTY WEIGHT: 23,450lb
MAX OVERLOAD: 36,200lb
MAX SPEED (WEP): 366mph at 20,000ft
INITIAL CLIMB RATE: 2,090 ft/min
RANGE: 1,350 miles at 229mph using long range cruise power

P-61 Black Widow

P-61A-1-NO Black Widow 42-5507 of 419th NFS was deployed to the South Pacific in February 1943 and was operational by April at Buka Airfield, Bougainville, Solomon Islands. Note the remote control General Electric dorsal turret fitted with four 0.5in, which combined with the four 20mm directly below in the ventral position, made a formidable field of fire. 42-5507 was lost 'somewhere' in the South Pacific on 10 April 1945.

P-61 BLACK WIDOW VARIANTS

(XP-61) two prototypes with R-2800-10 engines; (YP-61) 13 service test aircraft with R-2800-10 engines; (P-61A) 200 production aircraft, from 38th aircraft onwards, no dorsal turret was fitted, from 46th aircraft, water-injection R-2800-65 engine installed; (P-61B) production aircraft with R-2800-65 engines, majority built with pylons and dorsal turret, 450 built; (P-61C) production aircraft with 2,800hp (WEP) R-2800-73 engines with CH-5 turbochargers, Curtiss paddle-blade hollow steel propellers, capable of 430mph, only 41 delivered before order cancelled on VJ Day; (XP-61D) two P-61As re-engined with R-2800-77 turbocharged radials; (XP-61E) two P-61Bs re-built with slim nacelles, four 0.5in machine guns in place of radar in nose, pilot and navigator under bubble hood, increased internal fuel; (XP-61F) one P-61C to be modified as P-61E but never finished; (P-61G) 16 aircraft converted to weather reconnaissance/meteorological research; (XF-15 Reporter) first XP-61E rebuilt without armament and fitted with six aerial cameras; (XF-15A) a P-61C with a F-15 nacelle; (F-15A Reporter) production aircraft based on part-complete P-61C airframes, 36 built; (F2T-1N) surplus P-61As used as night fighter trainers by the United States Marine Corps (USMC) 12 aircraft transferred.

Bristol Beaufighter

Bristol's Wings for Victory Week in April 1943 was celebrated with Beaufighter VIF JL581, which had served with No 235 Squadron at Leuchars. It was lost after an engine failure on take-off and crashed near Gifford, East Lothian, on 5 May 1944, while with No 131 Operational Training Unit (OTU).

BRISTOL BEAUFIGHTER

The Bristol Beaufighter was a private venture development of the Beaufort torpedo-bomber using the latter's wings, tail and undercarriage mated to a new fuselage and more powerful engines. Designed as a long-range escort fighter, it first served as a night fighter with considerable success, and later excelled in the anti-shipping role equipped with torpedoes and rockets in addition to its four 20mm cannon and six machine guns.

The prototype, R2052, flew on 12 July 1939, and full production followed, early examples reaching Nos 25 and 604 Squadrons at North Weald and Middle Wallop, respectively, with others following including long-range coastal patrol fighters for Coastal Command.

Tropicalised Beaufighters operated in the Mediterranean and Middle East theatres, and when production ended in September 1945, a total of 5,564 had been built in England and 364 in Australia. In wartime, 46 squadrons used the type; post-war, it continued in service with several units, its final use being as a target-tug in Singapore where the last flight was operated by TT.X RD761 on 12 May 1960.

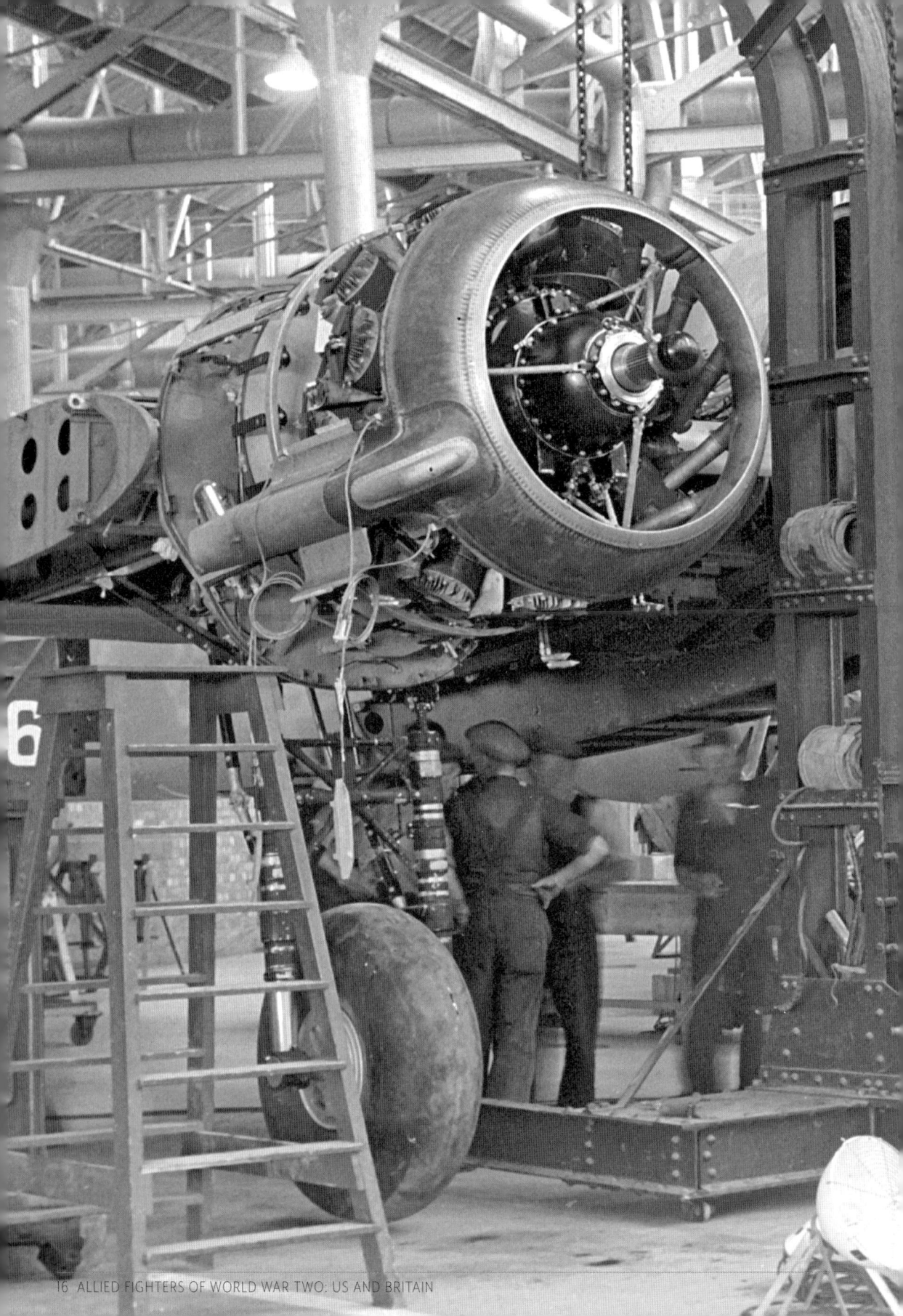

Early production of Beaufighters reveals the aircraft's size in comparison to Bristol's factory workers. In the foreground are four radar scanners awaiting installation.

Preparations for the installation of the Hercules engines.

Bristol Beaufighter

Loading a torpedo on to a Beaufighter. The Monoplane Air Tail (MAT) attachment was designed to stabilise it on release.

Ground crew loading 20mm cannon shells in ammunition boxes.

Loading one of eight 60lb rockets, carried on rails beneath each wing.

Bristol Beaufighter

A peaceful scene among the olive trees at Cassibile, Sicily, in 1943, with a Beaufighter VIF of No 600 Squadron receiving attention. The engines and area behind the cockpit are covered to resist the sun.

Bristol Beaufighter

Main: The navigator's position had a few basic instruments – this view faces towards the rear.

Below: The Beaufighter's cockpit was larger than that of single-seat fighters, but still compact.

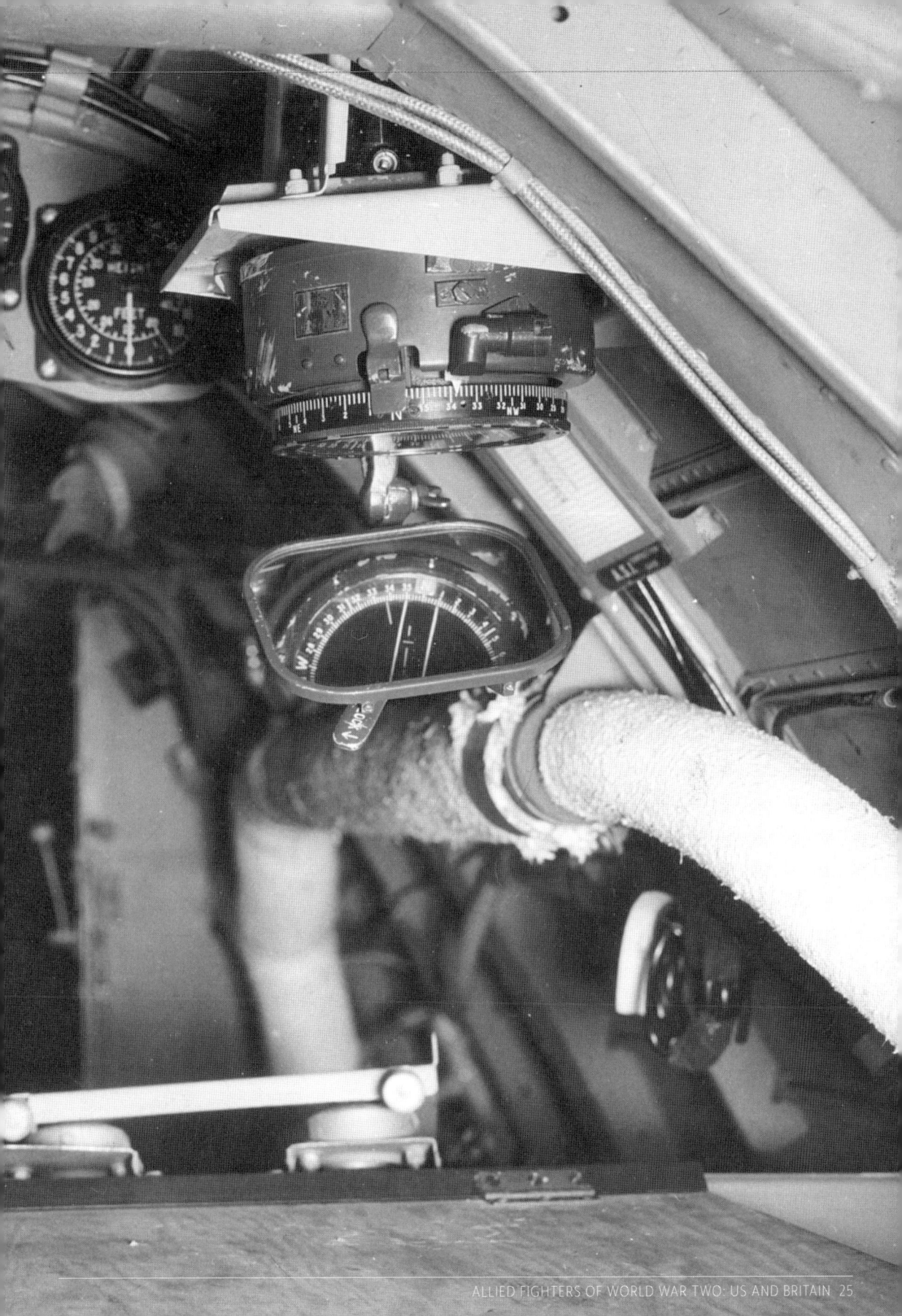

Bristol Beaufighter

A Beaufighter TF.X at the moment of landing – note the flaps and the puff of smoke from the port undercarriage wheel and the dihedral tailplane added to later production aircraft.

Production Beaufighter II T3177 was fitted with 1,720hp Rolls-Royce Griffon IIB engines for trials but nothing came of these and it became 4539M on 13 February 1944.

Beaufighter IIF T3019 at Filton in 1940 fitted with AI Mk IV radar. It served with No 307 Squadron at Exeter for a time but was written-off in a crash-landing in Berwickshire on 11 June 1942.

In its role as a target-tug, Beaufighter TT.X RD761 ended the type's RAF service on 12 May 1960, with a flight over Singapore from its base at Seletar, and was finally struck off charge eight days later.

Bristol Beaufighter

Unleashing eight 60lb rockets in a demonstration over The Wash is Beaufighter TF.X NE543 of 455 Squadron, Royal Australian Air Force (RAAF) based at Langham, Norfolk.

BRISTOL BEAUFIGHTER
ENGINES: Two 1,600hp Bristol Hercules (Mk VI)
WINGSPAN: 57ft 10in
LENGTH: 41ft 8in
HEIGHT: 15ft 10in
LOADED WEIGHT: 21,600lb
MAX SPEED: 333mph

CURTISS P-36 AND HAWK 75 FAMILY

When the Curtiss Model 75 first appeared in April 1935, it not only represented a pivotal moment in the history of Curtiss but also the US fighter aircraft industry as a whole. Designed by Donovan Reese Berlin, the Model 75 drew nothing from Curtiss' long experience in designing and building fighter aircraft. The fighter was a low-wing cantilever monoplane with an aluminium alloy semi-monocoque fuselage, multi-spar all-metal wing, both covered in Alclad knitted together with flush rivets. A retractable undercarriage, hydraulically actuated flaps and a fully enclosed cockpit with an aft opening canopy were features of the Model 75 which made it a state of the art machine and one of the most advanced fighters of its day. However, fighter development across the world began to accelerate from the mid-1930s, and within two years of the Model 75 entering service, certain aspects of its performance were already inferior. Highly manoeuvrable with pleasant handling characteristics, the Model 75 soon lacked the vital climb-and-dive, acceleration and level speed that would split the men from the boys during the early stages of World War Two.

Despite losing a US Army pursuit competition against the Seversky P-35, Curtiss would sell more Model 75s in the long run, 277 were sold to the USAAC as P-36s alone. Another 753, designated as the Hawk 75A, were sold overseas, the biggest

CURTISS HAWK 75-A4 (MOHAWK IV)
FIRST FLIGHT: December 1938
ENGINE: One 1,200hp Pratt & Whitney GR-1820-G205A (R-1820-97)
WINGSPAN: 37ft 4in
LENGTH: 28ft 7¾in
MAX SPEED: 323mph at 15,000ft
CLIMB RATE: 2,820ft/min
ARMAMENT: Six 0.5in FN Browning Mle 38 with 600rpg or six .303in Browning machine guns

order coming from France for 300 (later rising to 316) aircraft. France ordered the Hawk 75A with a Pratt & Whitney Twin Wasp engine (A-1 to A-3) and a Wright Cyclone powerplant (A-4). Many aircraft did not reach France before it fell in June 1940 and these were transferred to the RAF as the Mohawk Mk III (Wasp) and Mohawk Mk IV (ex-A4 Cyclone).

Eventually, 236 Mohawks entered RAF service from December 1914 when 5 Squadron was re-equipped at Dum Dum, Calcutta. 146 and 155 Squadrons (until January 1944) also operated the Mohawk in the Far East, as did 3 and 41 South African Air Force (SAAF) Squadrons in North Africa.

In French service, the II/4 Groupe de Chasses was credited with scoring the first Allied victories of World War Two when two Bf 109Es were brought down on 8 September 1939. Those machines that survived the German invasion were later used by the Vichy French in North Africa where they suffered heavy losses. In USAAC service, the P-36A joined the 20th Pursuit Group at Barksdale Field in April 1938 but a catalogue of teething problems put paid to the type's career at a very early stage. Relegated to training duties, a batch of 39 P-36As was delivered to Hawaii by the USS *Enterprise* in February 1941. Five of this group managed to get airborne during the Pearl Harbor attack, shooting down a pair of A6M2 Zeros for the loss of one P-36A. These were among the earliest US airborne victories of World War Two.

Originally ordered by the USAAC as a P-36A, 38-191 was delivered as a P-36C, a variant that featured an extra .30in machine gun in each wing and external ammunition boxes below the wing. This aircraft was written off on 18 March 1943, four miles east of El Paso, Texas.

Curtiss P-36 and Hawk 75 family

Rows of Curtiss Hawk 75s awaiting delivery to the French Air Force in 1939. A total of 100 H75-A1s, 100 H75H-2s, 60 H75-A3s (135 ordered) and just six H75-A4s (795 ordered) reached France before the country surrendered in June 1940.

THE CURTISS MODEL 75 FAMILY

(Model 75) prototype registered X-17Y; (Model 75A) company demonstrator; (Model 75A-1 [RAF Mohawk I]) first production batch for France designated in France as the H75C-1 (C = Chasse and the '1' = single-seater); (Model 75A-2 [RAF Mohawk II]) second batch for France with six 7.5mm machine guns; (Model 75A-3 [RAF Mohawk III]) third batch for France with improved 1,200hp R-1830-SIC3G engine and same armament as H75A-2; (Model 75A-4 [RAF Mohawk IV]) final batch for France, only 81 of 285 built reached France, remainder to RAF; (Model 75A-5 [RAF Mohawk IV]) originally to be built in China but transferred to India instead; (Model 75A-6) for Norway but captured by Germans and sold to Finland; (Model 75-A7) with Cyclone engines, ordered by Netherlands to serve in East Indies; (Model 75A-9 [RAF Mohawk IV]) intended for Persia but taken over by RAF and transferred to India; (Model 75-A8 [USAAC P-36G]) extra order from Norway, only six delivered, remaining 30 to USAAC and then Peru; (Model 75-A9 [RAF Mohawk IV]) for Persia but taken over by RAF to serve in India; (Model 75B) prototype with R-1820-G5 Cyclone engine; (Model 75D) the SCR-1670-5 powered XP-36 first prototype; (Model 75E) designated Y1P-36 by the USAAC; (Model 75H) export version with fixed undercarriage, one to China, one to Argentina; (Model 75I) Allison-powered XP-37 series with cockpit set further aft; (Model 75J) Model 75A with an external supercharger; (Model 75K) unbuilt R-2180 Twin Hornet-powered project; (Model 75L) designated as the P-36A (later P-36F) in USAAC service with an additional four .30in machine guns in wings; (Model 75M) production version of the Model 75H for China with retractable undercarriage; (Model 75N) non-retractable, similar to 75M for Siam; (Model 75O) non-retractable for Argentina; (Model 75P) re-engined P-36A with an Allison V-1710, this was the prototype XP-40 serialled 38-10; (Model 75Q) two non-retractable demonstrators; (Model 75R) Model 75A/75J demonstrator with an R-1830-SC2-G engine plus turbo-supercharger, beaten by Seversky XP-41 in 1939 US Army fighter competition; (Model 75S) USAAC XP-42; (P-36B) P-36A 38-20 temp designation to evaluate 8:1 supercharger; (P-36C) last 30 production P-36As fitted with an extra .30in machine gun and under wing ammunition boxes; (XP-36D) P-36A 38-174 with standard nose armament and four .30in machine guns in wings as per H75A-2; (XP-36E) P-36A 38-147 fitted with six .30in machine guns in wings; (XP-36F) P-36A 38-172 fitted with a pair of 23mm Madsen cannons under wings; (XP-37) rebuilt Model 75 prototype serialled 37-375; (YP-37) Model 75I fitted with an Allison V-1710 engine.

Curtiss P-36 and Hawk 75 family

Curtiss P-36Cs of the 27th Pursuit Squadron (PS), 1st FG pictured en route to the National Air Races at Cleveland, Ohio, in early September 1939. The unit only operated the type during 1939 and the unusual 'non-standard' pre-war camouflage was applied for war games that had only taken place a few weeks earlier.

Boulton Paul Defiant

BOULTON PAUL DEFIANT

The Boulton Paul Defiant was designed to Specification F.9/35 as the RAF's first (and only) single-engined fighter with a four-gun turret to enter service. Prototype K8310 flew on 11 August 1937 and the first production aircraft, L6950 (to revised Specification F.3/37), followed on 30 July 1939. First deliveries were in December 1939 to No 264 Squadron, Sutton Bridge, which saw action over Dunkirk in May 1940, but lack of forward-firing armament soon led to heavy losses.

Comparing loaded weights of the Defiant I (8,350lb) with two crew and a heavy turret and the single-seat Hurricane I (6,600lb), both with the same 1,030hp Rolls-Royce Merlin engine, one can see why the Defiant suffered, but it began to make its mark when transferred to night fighting. No 141 Squadron claimed the first victim, with Nos 255, 256 and 264 following, but Defiant night fighters were finally withdrawn in September 1942, being replaced by Mosquitoes and Beaufighters. They continued in support roles with air-sea rescue and anti-aircraft co-operation units and gunnery schools, a number being used as target-tugs until final retirement in April 1945. Total production reached 1,060.

The Defiant production line at the Boulton Paul factory, Wolverhampton, in February 1942. The lead aircraft already has its Rolls-Royce Merlin engine installed and main undercarriage fitted.

Boulton Paul Defiant

Defiant I N1550 was converted to the prototype Mk II and first flew on 20 June 1940, ignominiously taxiing into N1639 a week later. Following repair, it was fitted with this large tropical air cooler and went to the Aeroplane & Armament Experimental Establishment (A&AEE) at Boscombe Down for trials.

BOULTON PAUL DEFIANT
ENGINE: One 1,030hp Rolls-Royce Merlin III
WINGSPAN: 39ft 4in
LENGTH: 35ft 4in
HEIGHT: 12ft 2in
LOADED WEIGHT: 8,350lb
MAX SPEED: 303mph

Boulton Paul Defiant

A Defiant gunner of No 264 Squadron prepares to enter his turret – no easy task when wearing his parachute and protective clothing!

One of the turrets prior to fitting to the aircraft.

This Defiant target-tug in the markings of No 286 Squadron shows the winch operator's clear-vision canopy in place of the turret, and the drogue storage container beneath the fuselage. Many Defiants were used by the RAF and Royal Navy (RN) in this role in the UK and overseas, although operations in the tropics suffered with the plywood retractable fairings delaminating.

Boulton Paul Defiant

In night fighter black, Defiant I T4037/JT-T belonged to No 256 Squadron, which had re-formed at Catterick in November 1940. The fairings between cockpit and turret and between turret and fin are retracted to enable a wide field of fire. Subsequently serving with No 287 Squadron at Croydon, an anti-aircraft co-operation unit, it was struck off charge on 21 December 1944.

Defiant II AA436/DZ-V of No 151 Squadron, Wittering, in 1941 with the pilot's canopy open, turret guns pointing skyward and the rear fairing behind the turret retracted. Note the large forward ventral mast. This Defiant served with No 515 Squadron and No 1692 Radar Development Flight before being scrapped in June 1948.

Boulton Paul Defiant

The gunner is seen here doing his pre-flight checks, prior to entering the turret.

GLOSTER GLADIATOR

The Gladiator prototype, designated SS.37, was constructed using a modified Gauntlet fuselage and flew on 12 September 1934, becoming K5200. Named Gladiator on 1 July 1935, it was soon in production and deliveries to the RAF began on 16 February 1937, with No 72 Squadron at Tangmere being the first recipient. The type eventually served with 19 RAF squadrons in the UK and 15 overseas, while others of the 490 delivered equipped various Flights. Two squadrons were with the Advanced Air Striking Force in France in 1940, and during the Battle of Britain, No 247 Squadron's Gladiators defended Plymouth dockyards, while others operated from frozen lakes in Norway.

The Fleet Air Arm (FAA) received 60 specially built Sea Gladiators and 38 converted from RAF stocks. These served in 15 squadrons and four became famous in the defence of Malta. The last operational Gladiators were withdrawn in September 1941, but others served in RAF roles, notably meteorological reconnaissance, until 1945.

The fourth production Gladiator, K6132, had the more powerful 830hp Mercury IX engine, giving an increase in speed of 17mph to 253mph and a ceiling up from 10,000ft to 14,500ft. The cantilever undercarriage featured Dowty internally sprung wheels.

Gloster Gladiator

Early Gladiators were fitted with a two-bladed wooden propeller, while later models had three-bladed metal props. Clearly visible here are the flaps on top and bottom wings.

The Gloster SS.37 K5200, built to Specification F.7/30 for a four-gun fighter, taxies out at the SBAC Flying Display on 1 July 1935, when the name Gladiator was bestowed. It had a 530hp Bristol Mercury IV engine initially, later a 830hp Mercury, and was the RAF's last biplane fighter.

A fully equipped pilot must have had difficulty in entering a Gladiator cockpit, as shown here with a No 72 Squadron aircraft. Note the underwing Browning guns.

The Gladiator cockpit.

Gloster Gladiator

GLOSTER GLADIATOR
ENGINE: One 830hp Bristol Mercury IX
WINGSPAN: 32ft 3in
LENGTH: 27ft 5in
HEIGHT: 10ft 4in
LOADED WEIGHT: 4,750lb
MAX SPEED: 253mph

Another view of the fourth production Gladiator, K6132, which was delivered to No 72 Squadron at Tangmere on 22 February 1937.

Gloster Gladiator

Gladiators of No 87 Squadron, Debden, formation-keeping while linked together. No 87 received its first aircraft in June 1937 and re-equipped with Hurricanes in July 1938.

Gloster Gladiator

Gladiators of No 54 Squadron, Hornchurch, delivered in May 1937, two of which have their pilot's gear on the tailplane. The dark coloured fin on K7923 implies this has just been painted in a flight leader's colour.

In early 1939, seven Gladiators (N5590–5594, 5620–5621) were delivered to the Air Ministry's Meteorological Flight, Aldergrove. This example in camouflage, N5592, later passed to No 3 Bombing and Gunnery School and 402 Flight (a renaming of the Met Flight) – all based at Aldergrove – before crashing in a forced-landing in fog at Lady Hill, Co Antrim, on 6 September 1941.

The RN received several ex-RAF Gladiators before its two batches of Sea Gladiators, totalling 110. This is N5525, delivered to No 36 Maintenance Unit (MU) in March 1939 and sent to Malta the following month. Serving with No 802 Squadron on HMS *Glorious*, it was lost when the carrier was sunk by the *Scharnhorst* and *Gneisenau* on 8 June 1940, and the squadron ceased to exist.

HAWKER HURRICANE

The Hawker Hurricane was a private venture to meet Specification F.5/34, revised to F.36/34, and the prototype, K5083, flew on 6 November 1935. An initial contract for 600 was increased to 1,000 in November 1938 and the first production aircraft, L1547, flew on 12 October 1937, incorporating some revisions. Early versions had two-bladed fixed-pitch wooden propellers and fabric-covered fuselage and wings, later superseded by three-bladed metal props and metal-stressed-skin wings.

First deliveries went to No 111 Squadron, Northolt, in December 1937, while in March 1938, No 3 Squadron, Kenley, began to re-equip, the Hurricanes replacing Gauntlets and Gladiators.

The Hurricane and Spitfire Battle of Britain roles are, of course, legendary, and both went on to be developed into various versions. Each type had its advantages, the Hurricane proving to be quicker to repair when battle-damaged, while the Spitfire had performance edge.

Hurricanes, originally with eight machine guns, were later fitted with 12, then four-cannon versions, a tank-buster, night fighter and fighter-bomber. Production reached 12,711 in Britain and more than 1,400 in Canada and the type served with nearly 150 RAF and Commonwealth squadrons, while Sea Hurricanes equipped 19 FAA squadrons.

Hurricane Z4791/H-33, Spitfire Is P7882 and P7926/3 of the Empire Central Flying School (EFCS) Hullavington in October 1942, all with canopies open. The Hurricane was struck off charge in November 1944, Spitfire P7882 crashed at Hibaldstow on 9 May 1944, and P7926 was struck off charge in October 1944. The EFCS was redesignated the Empire Flying School (EFS) in May 1946.

Hawker Hurricane

The prototype Hurricane, K5083, during an early test flight. Following flight trials, during which it flew just over 153 hours, it became maintenance airframe 1211M in January 1939.

The first production Hurricane, L1547, flew on 12 October 1937, with some modifications from the prototype, the most obvious being removal of the tailplane bracing struts, but early deliveries lacked the ventral fairing around the tailwheel.

Canadian-built Hurricane XII RCAF 5624 was one of two fitted with streamlined skis developed by Noorduyn Aviation for the Harvard. The skis were fitted by Canadian Car & Foundry, Fort William, the wheel wells were covered and the undercarriage hydraulic system connected to ski trimming jacks. Although satisfactory, no further fittings were undertaken.

An armourer loads ammunition belts into a Hurricane I's machine guns in December 1939.

Hawker Hurricane

Hurricanes of No 111 Squadron being shown to the Press in March 1938. The squadron, which had operated Gloster Gauntlets from June 1936, became the first unit to be equipped with high-performance monoplanes and became a showpiece for the Press, MPs and other officials.

HAWKER HURRICANE
ENGINE: One 1,030hp Rolls-Royce Merlin II
WINGSPAN: 40ft 0in
LENGTH: 31ft 5in
HEIGHT: 13ft 1in
LOADED WEIGHT: 6,600lb
MAX SPEED: 316mph

Hawker Hurricane

Hurricane P3582 and others under repair in July 1940. It had a short life, serving with Nos 605 and 501 Squadrons before being abandoned near Folkestone on 15 August 1940, after being damaged by return fire from a Junkers Ju 87.

Hawker Hurricane

King George VI inspecting a No 111 Squadron Hurricane at Northolt in May 1938 while the CO, Sqn Ldr J. W. Gillan, AFC, explains the finer points. On 10 February, Gillan had flown a Hurricane from Edinburgh to Northolt in 48 minutes at more than 400mph – there was a tail wind!

Hawker Hurricane

Presentation Hurricane IIC KW924 *British Prudence* complete with pilot and 44-gallon long-range tanks ready to go. It had no RAF service, going to No 3 Squadron SAAF, and was struck off charge on 26 July 1945.

Hawker Hurricane

Pilots and dogs with the Hurricanes of No 3 Squadron, Kenley, in 1938. The Hurricanes were only operated for a short time as Kenley was deemed to be too small for them, and No 3 returned to Gladiators. However, Hurricanes were seen again at Kenley during the Battle of Britain.

Hawker Hurricane

Just about to re-equip with Typhoons in summer 1942, No 1 Squadron at Tangmere put up this flight of Hurricane IICs with a mixture of large and small serials. The nearest (and oldest) is Z3778, which crashed while overshooting at Acklington on 14 August 1942.

A-36A APACHE (AKA INVADER)

During 1941, the USAAF was expanding so quickly that there was not enough money in the kitty for new fighters. There was, however, money for attack aircraft and, after intensive discussions between the Pentagon and North American Aviation (NAA), the Mustang was redesigned for this role. The new aircraft was designated the NA-97 and, after an order for 500 aircraft (42-83663–84162) was placed on 21 August 1942, it was officially referred to as the A-36A, which was basically a dive-bomber version of the Mustang.

The first A-36A took to the air in the hands of NAA test pilot Ben Chilton on 21 September 1942. Power was provided by an Allison V-1710-87 (F21R) engine, which was rated at 1,325hp at 3,000ft. The aircraft was stressed for high-speed diving and a set of fence-type hydraulically operated dive brakes were fitted above and below each wing. Positioned outboard of the bomb hardpoints, the dive brakes were recessed into the wing but were opened to 90° by a hydraulic jack to hold speed in very steep dives at around the 350mph mark.

Armament was a pair of 0.5in Brownings in each wing and another pair in the nose, although the latter fit was often deleted in the field to save weight. Under each wing was a pair of racks to carry either a pair of 500lb bombs, smoke generators or a pair of 75-US gallon drop tanks.

Flight tests were carried out at Eglin Army Air Field in Florida and it was quickly discovered that the A-36 could easily achieve a dive speed of 500mph. With the dive breaks extended, this

The keen-eyed will notice the twin-landing lights in front of the retracted speed brakes, both of which were unique to the NA-97, more commonly known as the A-36. A total of 500 of these dive-bombing/ground-attack machines were built, all working hard in the Mediterranean and Far East well into 1944.

A-36A *"Bronx Cheer"* of the 27th Bomber Group (BG) gives a nice view of the dive brakes extended and a pair of 500lb bombs in place. Other features of the variant are the early type flame-damping exhausts and early style bomb shackles.

A-36A Apache (aka Invader)

was reduced to 350mph but, unfortunately, one of the early test aircraft was lost when both wings came off in a vertical dive. This incident sowed some seeds of doubt amongst certain Army officials who acknowledged that while the A-36 had an excellent dive rate for a fighter, it went down too fast for a dive-bomber. It was recommended that the A-36 be restricted to a dive angle of 70° and that it should be used mainly as a low-altitude attack aircraft with the dive brakes removed. The latter recommendation was never implemented.

One of the many challenges the fledgling A-36 pilot had to face was the distinct lack of specialist training available at the time in dive bombing techniques. A handful of US Navy (USN) and United States Marine Corps (USMC) instructors were temporarily loaned to the Army but it was generally an art that was initially self-taught through experience and improvisation. A distinct lack of aircraft was another problem, with many A-36 pilots only encountering the type once they were in theatre because none were available during their training. Replacement aircraft were also lacking but what the A-36 is rarely credited for is the fact that it kept the production lines open for the Merlin engine variants that were to come later and would accelerate the Mustang into a classic fighter.

It was not until late March 1943 that the A-36A-1-NA began to enter the USAAF, the first recipients being the four squadrons of the 27th Fighter-Bomber Group (FBG) based at Rasel Ma in French Morocco. Not long after, a second group, the 86th FBG,

Ex-42-83685 was the only A-36A to arrive in Britain during World War Two. Re-serialled as EW998, the aircraft arrived at Boscombe Down on 10 March 1943. It was prematurely struck off charge on 15 July 1943.

arrived and had a full contingent of fully qualified A-36 pilots on board. In this theatre of war, the A-36 was referred to as the Invader, despite the fact that its official name was the Apache, the name rejected by the RAF in favour of the Mustang.

The first operational sorties were flown on 6 June 1943, against the island of Pantelleria. Following the massed fighter-bomber attack, the island was captured and became home to a pair of A-36 groups, which would go on to take part in the invasion of Sicily.

Post-war statistics compiled by the USAAF on the A-36A revealed that the type flew more 23,000 sorties and, despite being a ground attack aircraft, claimed 86 enemy aircraft destroyed in air-to-air combat.

A-36A

ENGINE: (P-51A) One 1,325hp Allison V-1710-87 (F21R)
WINGSPAN: 37ft 1¼in
LENGTH: 32ft 2½in
HEIGHT: 8ft 8in
EMPTY WEIGHT: 8,370lb
LOADED WEIGHT: 10,700lb
MAX SPEED: 365mph
SERVICE CEILING: 25,100ft
RANGE: 550 miles with full load

A-36A Apache (aka Invader)

An A-36A of the 86th Fighter-Bomber Group (FBG), in Italy in 1944 with two enemy aircraft to its credit, being serviced in typical field conditions.

LOCKHEED P-38 LIGHTNING

The Lockheed P-38 Lightning was the innovative result of a far sighted proposal that was issued for a twin-engined interceptor in 1936. This concept of the twin-engined fighter was simultaneously explored by Britain, France and Germany but the P-38 would emerge as the only plausible design and certainly the only one to achieve, amongst many other things, massed production.

Unique from every angle, the P-38, designed by Hall L. Hibbard and Clarence 'Kelly' Johnson, was also the world's first fighter to be fitted with a nose wheel undercarriage; the first single-seat fighter with twin booms to enter service; the first fighter to be installed with turbo-superchargers; the first fighter to have power-boosted controls (from the P-38J onwards); and the first aircraft in the world to encounter the new phenomenon of compressibility.

First flown on 27 January 1939, the prototype XP-38 was followed by a pre-production order of 13 YP-38s, ordered on 27 April, and a further order for 66 production P-38s. Thirty P-38s were actually delivered, the remainder of the order being 36 P-36D Lightnings (only from this mark was that name adopted), the first fully combat ready version of the fighter. Deliveries commenced from August 1941. An impressive order for 622 aircraft was placed by the RAF as Model 222s but the first three aircraft that were received had not been fitted with turbo-superchargers so the order was cancelled and later diverted to USAAF contracts. It was the P-38E, with a 20mm instead of a 37mm cannon in the nose, and the more powerful P-38F that took the USAAF into World War Two, although it was actually an F-4 (reconnaissance variant of the P-38E) armed with K17 cameras that entered

active service with the 8th Photographic Squadron (PS) in Australia from April 1942.

The first blood for the P-38 came on 14 August 1942, when a P-38F of the 1st FG based in Iceland finished off an Fw 200 Condor over the Atlantic. By late 1942, the P-38 began to arrive in North Africa for service with the 12th Air Force and support of Operation *Torch*. By 1943, the P-38 was being progressively transferred to the 8th and later 9th Air Force in Britain where it performed well in its intended role as a long-range escort fighter until replaced by the P-51. The P-38 also arrived in the Pacific theatre from late 1942 and, by the end of the war, had downed more than 1,800 Japanese aircraft and over 100 pilots had achieved Ace status.

LOCKHEED P-38J LIGHTNING

FIRST FLIGHT: (XP-38) 27 January 1939
ENGINE: Two 1,425hp (at 28,500ft) Allison V-1710-89/91
WINGSPAN: 52ft
LENGTH: 37ft 10in
MAX SPEED: 360mph at 5,000ft
CLIMB RATE: 3,670 ft/min
Armament: One 20mm AN-M2 'C' cannon and four 0.50in machine guns

The P-38 matured into one of World War Two's greatest multi-role aircraft, capable of all forms of aerial warfare ranging from escort fighter to ground attack aircraft, or a dive-bomber, night fighter or a photo reconnaissance machine. With nearly 10,000 built, the P-38 broke all the rules but served the US from Pearl Harbor to VJ Day.

Lockheed P-38 Lightning

Above: Thousands of female employees were taken on by all of the world's aircraft manufacturers during the World War Two. Lockheed was no exception and included this young lady, who was working on a P-38 at Burbank, California, in 1944.

Main: P-38G-10-LO Lightnings of the 344th FS, 343rd FG, based at Fort Randall, Alaska, which, up to October 1943, was flying operational missions against the Japanese in P-40s. The unit was deactivated in 1946.

LOCKHEED P-38 LIGHTNING VARIANTS

(XP-38) the prototype; (YP-38) 13 evaluation aircraft; (P-38) 30 production aircraft; (XP-38A) a single variant with a pressurised cockpit; (P-38D) fitted with self-sealing fuel tanks and armoured windshield, 'combat-ready', 36 built; (P-38E) improved instruments, electrical and hydraulic system, 37mm cannon replaced by 20mm Hispano autocannon; extra ammunition capacity, 210 built (99 to F-4s); (Model 322) three aircraft for RAF; (RP-322) trainer, 147 built; (P-38F) installed with racks inboard of engines for drop tanks or 2,000lb of bombs, 'combat manoeuvre' setting added to Fowler flaps, 527 built; (F-4A) improved F-4 based on P-38F, 20 built; (P-38G) improved version of P-38F, 1,082 built; (F-5A) reconnaissance machine based on P-38G, 180 built; (XF-5D) a single converted F-5A; (P-38H) improved P-38G with an automatic cooling system, 601 built; (F-5C) reconnaissance version of the P-38H, 123 built; (P-38J) improved cooling and electrical systems, 2,970 built; (F-5B) reconnaissance version of the P-38J, 200 built; (F-5E) a conversion of the P-38J/L, 605 built; (P-38K) one aircraft modified with 1,425hp V-1710 engines and paddle blade props; (P-38L-LO) updated engines and new rocket pylons, 3,810 built; (P-38L-VN) built by Vultee, 113 built; (F-5F) reconnaissance version of the P-38L; (P-38M) 'Night Lightning' night fighter, 75 built; (F-5G) reconnaissance machine.

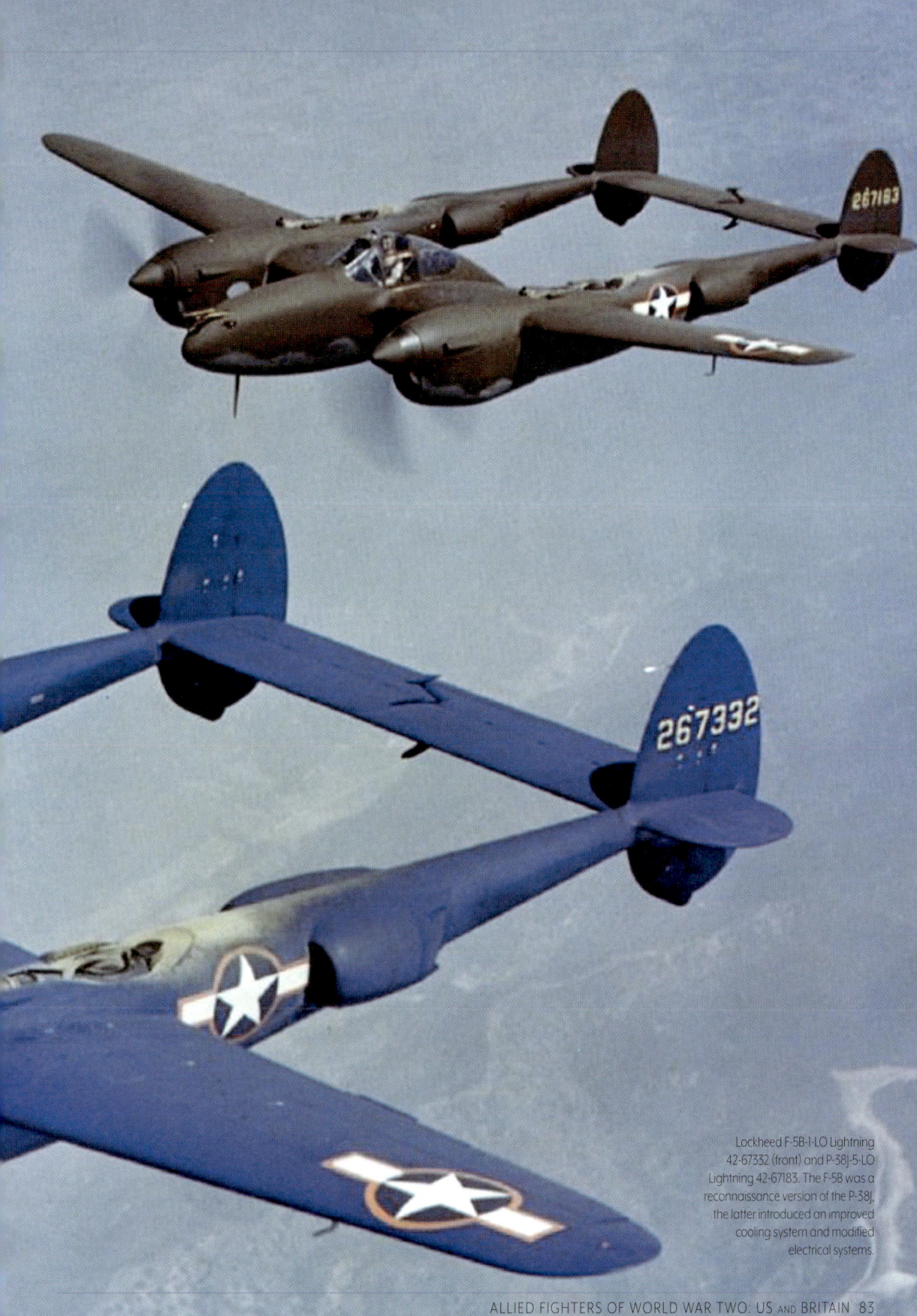

Lockheed F-5B-1-LO Lightning 42-67332 (front) and P-38J-5-LO Lightning 42-67183. The F-5B was a reconnaissance version of the P-38J, the latter introduced an improved cooling system and modified electrical systems.

CURTISS P-40D TO Q WARHAWK/KITTYHAWK I, IA, II, III AND IV

Following the introduction of the Allison V-1710-39 in early 1941, complete with an external-spur reduction, the following model, the P-40D, was six inches shorter than the earlier machines. It also gained a name, the Warhawk*, and not only was the airframe shorter, the forward fuselage cross-section was also deeper, the radiator was re-positioned and the main undercarriage was shortened. The nose guns were deleted and the wing guns were replaced with four 0.5in. Only 26 P-40Ds were built for the USAAC but 560 were manufactured for the RAF and named the Kittyhawk I. The first of these joined 112 Squadron in December 1941 and further deliveries were made to 94, 250, 260 and 450 Squadrons and 5 and 7 (SAAF) Squadrons and 3 (RAAF) Squadron.

The first large production variant was the P-40E with six 0.5in machine guns in the wings and a top speed that matched the Spitfire VC, although the British fighter was always more manoeuvrable. A total of 2,320 P-40Es were built, 1,500 of these were supplied to the RAF as the Kittyhawk IA, although a large number later served with RAAF, Royal New Zealand Air Force (RNZAF) and Royal Canadian Air Force (RCAF) units.

With large quantities of the Packard-built Merlin engine already in full swing by late 1941, the next variant of the Warhawk was selected for this powerplant. P-40D 40-360 was fitted with a Merlin 28 and redesignated as the XP-40F, which increased the weight to 9,460lb and raised the top speed to 383mph at 18,000ft. From the 260th production aircraft onwards, the P-40F's rear fuselage was lengthened by 20in, but a gradual increase in weight reduced the top speed to 364mph. In total, 1,311 P-40Es were built for the USAAF and a further 330 were converted for the RAF as the Kittyhawk II and IIA. The plan was to return these machines to the US at a later date, but in the end, only 80 were returned to the USAAF. The only other Merlin-powered variant was the P-40L, which was powered by the V-1650-1 and lightened to improve performance. By 1944, the P-51 was putting great demands on the Merlin and approximately 300 P-40Fs and P-40Ls were converted to take the Allison V-1710-81 and redesignated as the P-40R-1 and R-2 and used as trainers.

While P-40F production was underway, the P-40K, with a 1,325hp Allison V-1710-73, was introduced. A total

A P-40F Warhawk beats up a North African strip in 1943; the 'F' was the first variant to be fitted with the Merlin engine, which resulted in another nose change complete with an up draught trunk intake and revised ducting.

of 1,300 P-40Ks were built and the marginal increase in performance was sufficient to give them the edge over the Bf 109E over North Africa and the A6M in the Far East. The P-40M raised the horsepower bar slightly again by being fitted with a 1,360hp V-1710-81. There were 600 P-40Ms built for the USAAF, 16 of these were diverted to the RAF and a further 600 were delivered as the Kittyhawk III.

The definitive member of the Warhawk family was the P-40N, which entered production in late 1943 and entered USAAF service from March 1944. Powered by an Allison V-1710-81, the P-40N was lightened back down to 8,850lb, in part due to the removal of the forward fuselage fuel tank and to having just four machine guns in the wings. In total, 1,977 P-40N to N-15s were built, followed by the 3,023 P-40N-20 to N-35 with a V-1710-99 engine and six machine guns. A further 200 P-40N-40s were built and 588 were delivered to the RAF as the Kittyhawk IV serving with 112, 250 and 450 Squadrons.

Ground crew of the 57th FG, 9th AF in Tunisia service the machine guns of a P-40.

CURTISS P-40E

FIRST FLIGHT: (Model 87-A) 22 May 1941
ENGINE: One 1,150hp Allison V-1710-39
WINGSPAN: 37ft 4in
LENGTH: 31ft 9in
MAX SPEED: 362mph at 15,000ft
CLIMB RATE: 2,100 ft/min
Armament: Six .50in M2 Browning machine guns and up 2,000lb of bombs

*Some sources state that all P-40s were named Warhawk while others declare it was given this name from the 'D'.

Curtiss P-40D to Q Warhawk/Kittyhawk I, IA, II, III and IV

The Warhawk served the USAAF in virtually every theatre during World War Two. These included the 8th and 49th FG, 5th Air Force, in the Far East between 1942 and 1944, the 15th and 18th FG, 7th Air Force, the 'Hawaiian Air Force', between 1941 and 1944, the 57th and 79th FG, 9th Air Force, in the Mediterranean between 1942 and 1944, the 23rd FG and 51st PG, 10th Air Force, in India and Burma and the 27th and 33rd FG, 12th Air Force, also in the Mediterranean between 1942 and 1944. The Curtiss fighter also provided the backbone of the USAAF's fighter defences over the Panama Canal, serving with the 16th, 32nd, 36th, 37th and 53rd PG.

When production came to end in 1944, 13,738 P-40s had been built, making it the third most-produced fighter in America behind the P-51 and the P-47. Despite the fact that the P-40's overall performance was severely lacking by 1944, the type proved to still be a valuable asset in secondary theatres of war and to other air forces. The Soviet Union in particular actually received 2,425 aircraft (including 247 P-40C/Tomahawk IIB), all of which were originally purchased by Britain but diverted between 1942 and 1943. An order of 377 P-40s, the bulk of them P-40Ns, were sent to China and P-40Es to Brazil and Chile. While a few Warhawks remained in service in limited numbers with the USAAF, it was 120 Squadron, Netherlands Army Air Corp, which used the P-40N for the last time operationally in Indonesia during 1946 and 1947.

P-40F Warhawk 41-14274, which was later wrecked at Berteaux, Algeria, on 12 December 1943.

LATER P-40 VARIANTS

(P-40D [Model 87-A2]) V-1710-39 engine's spur reduction gear raised thrust-line which changed nose to a shorter design, nose guns omitted, 23 built named Warhawk; (P-40E [Model 87-B2]) six .50in machine guns and provision for six 20lb or a single 500lb bomb, 820 built; (P-40E-1 [Model 87-A4]) to identify 1,500 Kittyhawk IAs for Britain under Lend-Lease, many served with USAAF; (XP-40F [Model 87-B3]) one aircraft installed with a British-built 1,300hp Merlin 28 (first flown 30 June 1941), production aircraft fitted with Packard V-1650-1, no top-mounted carburettor scoop; (YP-40F) second prototype P-40F with various modifications; (P-40F) first 699 of 1,311 ordered had no dash numbers, F-5s onwards had a 20in fuselage extension to improve directional stability, F-10s had manual cowl flaps, F-15s were winterised and F-20s had updated oxygen systems, 150 delivered to Britain as the Kittyhawk II; (XP-40G) a P-40 with H81-A2 Tomahawk IIA wings with four .30in machine guns; (P-40G) 43 aircraft fitted with Tomahawk IIA wings, 16 were shipped to Soviet Union; (P-40K) 1,300 aircraft ordered with altitude-rated V-1710-73 engines; (P-40L [Model 87-B3]) 700 aircraft similar to P-40F-5, 100 delivered to Britain as Kittyhawk II; (P-40M) 600 aircraft were basically the same as the P-40K-20 but with a V-1710-81 engine, 364 delivered to Britain as Kittyhawk IIIs and 19 to Brazil; (P-40N [Model 87V & 87W]) 5,200 aircraft with various revisions; (XP-40Q [Model 87X]) two P-40Ks and a single P-40N modified with new cooling systems, superchargers and structural changes; (P-40R) approximately 600 P-40Fs and P-40Ls relegated to training duties; (TP-40) two-seat conversion of P-40N.

Curtiss P-40D to Q Warhawk/Kittyhawk I, IA, II, III and IV

A line of P-40Es of the 18th PG in the harsh environment of the Aleutian Islands.

Curtiss P-40K-1-CU Warhawk 42-46040, of the 64th FS, 57th FG, 9th Air Force, taxiing out for a bombing mission on an Egyptian field in 1943. Working closely with Allied units over North Africa, the 57th FG achieved a large number of successes against the enemy and was not re-equipped with the P-47 until early 1944.

GLOSTER METEOR

The Gloster Meteor stemmed from eight aircraft designated Gloster Whittle F.9/40 ordered in February 1941. The first, DG202/G, began taxi trials in July 1942, but delays in production of the original engine led to the first flight being made by the fifth aircraft, DG206/G, with de Havilland engines on 5 March 1943, by which time the name Meteor had been adopted.

Twenty Meteor F.Is were ordered, first deliveries on 12 July 1944 being to No 616 Squadron, Culmhead, which soon moved to Manston to combat the V1 flying-bombs. One Flight later moved to Belgium, making its first operational sortie on 17 April 1945, being used in the ground attack role. Its aircraft were given an overall white wash to avoid confusion with Messerschmitt Me 262s, but there were no jet-on-jet encounters.

Total production of Meteor F.Is reached 210, some 30 being used on development work such as ejector-seat trials. Meteor F.Is and IIIs served with 17 squadrons, continuing into the post-war period but were soon replaced by Mk 4s featuring more powerful engines and other improvements.

Meteor F.IIIs of No 257 Squadron, Horsham-St-Faith, being pushed out of the hangar for the day's flying. The squadron began to re-equip from Typhoons in September 1946, and EE253/A6-E had previously served with 616 Squadron, subsequently returning to that unit. It was scrapped in 1956.

This unusual overwash white scheme on F.III EE240 was used by a Flight from No 616 Squadron transferred to operate on the Continent with No 84 Group, 2nd Tactical Air Force and based at Nijmegen. The colour scheme was designed to inform trigger-happy Allied gunners that the Meteors were not Me 262s. This Meteor had a short life, becoming instructional airframe 5782M in January 1946.

Gloster Meteor

The Meteor F.III had a clear instrument panel with easy-to-read instruments. Note the undercarriage locks on the left and gunsight at top centre. The jettison hood lever is very obvious at the right of the main panel.

The port side cannon installation in an early Meteor, identified by the original type canopy.

Gloster Meteor

Meteor F.IIIs of No 245 Squadron, Colerne, one of the early squadrons to receive jets, converting from Typhoons in 1945. It continued to operate this mark until beginning to re-equip with Meteor F.8s in August 1950.

Gloster Meteor

A neat line-up of Meteor F.IIIs of No 74 Squadron, Colerne, in September 1945 when it formed the RAF's first jet fighter wing with Nos 616 and 504 Squadrons. For those who like details, those identifiable are EE346/4D-Z, EE306/4D-N, EE343/4D-X, EE333/4D-R and EE340/4D-T. The nearest, EE346, crashed near Chippenham on 19 July 1946, EE306 became 6966M, EE343 was lost in the North Sea in November 1946, EE333 crash-landed at Lubeck on 8 July 1947 and EE340, the longest-lived of these, was scrapped in June 1956.

GLOSTER METEOR IV
ENGINES: Two 3,500lb Rolls-Royce Derwent
WINGSPAN: 43ft 0in
LENGTH: 41ft 4in
HEIGHT: 13ft 0in
LOADED WEIGHT: 15,545lb
MAX SPEED: 585mph

DE HAVILLAND MOSQUITO

The de Havilland Mosquito prototype flew on 25 November 1940. The first night fighter prototype, W4076, flew on 15 May 1941, and the NF.II with AI Mk IV radar entered service with No 23 Squadron, Ford, in May 1942 and No 157 Squadron, Castle Camps, in August 1942.

Most widely used in the fighter-bomber role was the FB.VI, of which 2,718 were built by de Havilland, Standard Motors and Airspeed. It had four nose-mounted machine guns and four 20mm Hispano cannon, while later deliveries carried eight 60lb rockets mounted on rails beneath the wings. They equipped a large number of Fighter and Coastal Command squadrons in the UK and overseas, and total Mosquito production of all marks reached 7,781, including those built in Canada and Australia.

The pilot signing off a Mosquito FB.VI for the ground crew.

Emblazoned with 'invasion stripes', FB.VI NT225's nose armament was reduced to two .303 machine guns used for sighting the Molins six-pounder 57mm cannon visible beneath the nose. Two 100-gallon drop-tanks were necessary for long-range anti-shipping patrols.

De Havilland Mosquito

The de Havilland production line at Leavesden, showing part of a batch of 299 Mk FB XVIIs delivered between June and September 1943.

De Havilland Mosquito

Factory mechanics work on installing the port Merlin engine.

Far right: Wing manufacture.

Production of fighter-bomber versions, showing the stages from nine to one on the white boards along the assembly hall walls.

De Havilland Mosquito

The cockpit of a Mosquito fighter-bomber, note the open access door on the starboard side.

View from the cockpit during a formation. The relector gun sight (in centre) was used to line up with the target.

Servicing the armament of a Mosquito FB.VI, showing the ease of access.

De Havilland Mosquito

Mosquito F.IIs of No 264 Squadron at Predannack in April 1943. Formerly at Colerne, it had re-equipped from Defiants in 1942, and began to receive Mosquito FB.VIs in August 1943.

De Havilland Mosquito

Mosquito FB.VI HR405 of No 143 Squadron displays its underwing 25lb rockets and nose armament. The squadron's operational area was the Norwegian coast with strikes against shipping for which 25lb rockets were found more effective than the heavier 60lb version.

DE HAVILLAND MOSQUITO F.II
ENGINE: Two 1,460hp Rolls-Royce Merlin 21
WINGSPAN: 54ft 2in
LENGTH: 40ft 6in
HEIGHT: 12ft 6in
LOADED WEIGHT: 22,300lb
MAX SPEED: 380mph

XP-51, P-51, P-51A and Mustang II

XP-51, P-51, P-51A AND MUSTANG II

ENGINE: (XP-51 & P-51) One 1,150hp Allison V-1710-39 (F3R); (P-51A) One 1,200hp Allison V-1710-81 (F20R); (Mustang II) One 1,120hp Allison V-1710-81

WINGSPAN: 37ft 1¼in

LENGTH: 32ft 2½in

HEIGHT: 8ft 8in

LOADED WEIGHT: 8,600lb

MAX SPEED: (XP-51 & P-51) 390mph at 8,000ft; (P-51A) 409mph at 11,000ft; (Mustang II) 390mph at 8,000ft

XP-51, P-51, P-51A AND MUSTANG II

During the early stages of Mustang production, the fourth and tenth aircraft were allocated to the USAAC and designated as XP-51s on 24 July 1941. These two aircraft, 41-038 and 41-039, were selected for evaluation as part of the Army's fighter programme, which was already inundated with the new types put forward by Bell, Curtiss, Lockheed and Republic. The test pilots at Wright Field were overworked with testing products from companies that were already established in building fighter types. NAA was still an unknown quantity and would have to take its turn.

41-038 arrived at Wright Field on 24 August and remained until 22 December, which must have been an agonising amount of time for a new aircraft. The main reason for the delay, apart from the test pilots' work load, was that the P-51 was not designed for the USAAC and, as such, was not viewed as being a particularly important aircraft. The amount of time the aircraft took to evaluate was also causing concern in Britain to such an extent that a representative travelled to Wright Field to investigate the situation. It was found that each aircraft's project officer became so strongly involved with the evaluation that they became a sales representative for the manufacturer rather than working to find the best fighter for the USAAC.

The USAAC did order 148 P-51s (NA-91) Apaches on 7 July 1941, as part of a USAAF order well before testing began. This was on behalf of the RAF in a Lend-Lease deal, which was viewed as a top up order.

THE FASTEST OF THE ALLISON-ENGINED MUSTANGS
The USAAF ordered 310 NA-99s, designated the P-51A, in early 1942. Effectively, these aircraft were A-36As with the dive brakes and twin nose guns removed. The P-51A at medium height was the fastest fighter in the world and was also described as having 'the best all-round fighting qualities of any present American fighter'. Armament consisted of four 0.5in Brownings with large magazine tanks capable of holding up to 1,260 rounds. The ability to carry a pair of 500lb bombs or a pair of drop tanks was also retained.

The P-51A first flew on 3 February 1943 and, of the 310 P-51As built, 50 were sent to Britain as Mustang IIs, while the remainder were despatched to India and North Africa where they saw extensive action. The first, though, were sent to the 54th FG at Bartow Army Field, Florida, where new Mustang pilots would cut their teeth on the fighter.

The Mustang II first entered RAF service with 225 Squadron at Souk el Arba in Tunisia in April 1943. Operating alongside the Spitfire VB, the Mustang only served until July 1943 when it was replaced by the Spitfire VC. The final RAF operational unit to fly the Mustang II was 268 Squadron who received the type at B.70/Deurne in November 1944. Like 2 Squadron, the unit fought its way east towards Berlin and victory in Europe but did not part with its Mustangs until August 1945.

P-51B, P-51C AND MUSTANG III

After the first Mustangs arrived in Britain, the resulting testing of the Allison-powered Mk I by the RAF and Rolls-Royce test pilots revealed the fighter to be a very good aircraft. It also became clear that the Mustang was the ideal machine to take the outstanding Rolls-Royce Merlin engine, and this would improve the aircraft's medium to high altitude performance. Coincidentally, the engine was being produced in the US by the Packard Motor Company, under the designation V-1650.

The concept quickly came into fruition and, stateside, a pair of P-51s (NA-91), 41-37352 and 41-37421, were fitted with Packard-Merlin V-1650 engines. Initially designated as the XP-78 (NA-101), this was quickly changed to the XP-51B. In Britain, five prototypes were set aside for trials with Rolls-Royce at Hucknall from July 1942.

The modifications that were needed to transform the Allison-engined design into a Merlin-engined design were more extensive than first envisaged. A great deal of wind-tunnel testing was needed because the Merlin engine was over 350lb heavier than the Allison. A four-blade propeller added even more weight, which, along with the engine, changed the aircraft's weight and balance calculations by a great deal. A bigger radiator and modified cooling system was also needed and the intake for the Merlin's updraft carburettor had to be moved from above the forward fuselage to below it.

The first Merlin-powered Mustang, AL975/G, by then redesignated as the Mustang X, was flown by Capt R. T. Shepherd from Hucknall on 13 October 1942. In the US, Bob Chilton flew the first XP-51B on 30 November 1942. Both aircraft produced excellent performance figures, which, at altitude, were up to 100mph faster than the Allison-powered variant.

Prior to this, the USAAF had confidently ordered 400 P-51Bs and, by the time that the prototypes had been proven in the air, even more were required so both the Inglewood and Dallas factories were expanded to cope. Those aircraft that were built in California would be designated as the P-51B-NA and the Texan-built machines were designated as the P-51C-NT, while in British service the fighter would be known as the Mustang III.

The 354th FG, 9th Air Force, was the first unit to receive a Merlin-powered Mustang in October 1943. The group flew its first operation on 1 December and gained its first enemy kill on 15 December. The same month, 65 Squadron was the first RAF unit to re-equip with the Mustang III, which were initially used for bomber-escort duties while the USAAF built up its own inventory of P-51Bs and Cs.

While 9th Air Force units gained more P-51B/Cs, the 8th Air Force also began to receive the type from early 1944 and, from February, the 14th Air Force in Burma saw the type arrive. By April, the fighter also began to re-equip the 15th Air Force in the Mediterranean theatre.

The P-51B/C Mustang was an outstanding fighter aircraft and in many pilots' eyes was the definitive mark of the breed, despite the visibility advantages that the D-model would bring. The introduction of the Malcolm-type hood sought to rectify this one major issue with the P-51B/C.

The RAF received 946 Mustang IIIs in the serial ranges FB100–FB399, FX848–FX999, FZ100–FZ197, HB821–HB961, KH421–KH640 and SR406–SR440. This is FX893 during trials with A&AEE, Boscombe Down. Transferred to the Middle East, the fighter was struck off charge on 29 August 1946.

P-51B, P-51C AND MUSTANG III

ENGINE: (B) One 1,620hp Packard Merlin V-1650-3 12-cylinder Vee liquid-cooled; (C) One 1,695hp Packard Merlin V-1650-7 12-cylinder Vee liquid-cooled
WINGSPAN: 37ft ¼in
LENGTH: 32ft 3in
HEIGHT: 8ft 8in
MAX LOADED WEIGHT: (B) 11,200lb; (C) 11,800lb
MAX SPEED: (B) 440mph at 30,000ft; (C) 439mph at 25,000ft

P-51B AND P-51C PRODUCTION

Not including the RAF and NAA prototypes, 3,738 P-51B/Cs were built, of which 910 were delivered to the RAF as Mustang IIIs under Lend-Lease. A total of 91 aircraft were built for the USAAF as F-6Cs, fitted with a pair of aerial cameras and retaining the P-51B/C's standard 0.5in quartet of wing-mounted machine guns.

P-51B-15-NA Mustang 42-106950, of the 354th FS, 355th FG, with Lt Robert Hulderman at the controls during a sortie from Steeple Morden. Nicknamed the 'Steeple Morden Strafers', the 355th FG began receiving the Mustang, in place of the P-47, from the spring of 1944 onwards.

P-51B, P-51C & Mustang III

Above: Originally delivered to the RAF as Mustang III FX905, this P-51B-1NA was transferred to the USAAF on 20 December 1943, to serve with the 362nd FS, 357th FG, at Leiston. The P-51 was later transferred to the 359th FG before being declared 'war weary' to serve as a 'hack' with the 353rd FG at Raydon.

Main: The 376th FS, 361st FG, warm through their Merlin engines in the sunshine at Bottisham in June 1944 prior to another sortie over Northern France. Initially equipped with the P-47, the unit began to convert to the P-51B/C from May 1944 and, even after the arrival of the P-51D, the unit held onto its original aircraft until early 1945.

Capt Andrew D. Turner (left), and Lt Clarence P. Lester of the 332nd FG talk tactics at Ramitelli, Italy, in August 1944. The 332nd FG did not fly the P-51 until 1944.

P-51D, K AND MUSTANG IV

The ability to spot your enemy early was a crucial element for a fighter pilot and the most obvious weak point was from the rear. This problem was partly addressed through the introduction of the British-designed Malcolm hood, which was retrofitted to many P-51B, Cs and Mustang IIIs. The next model in the chain would solve this problem by introducing a bubble canopy that would give the pilot superb all-round vision.

Three P-51Bs, 43-12102, 42-106539 and 42-106540, were selected for conversion to D-model standard and the first of these flew on 17 November 1943, in the hands of Bob Chilton. The main conversion work involved lowering the rear fuselage contour, which was partly replaced by a dorsal fin to help maintain directional stability. The wing-root chord was also increased, the landing gear was made stronger and was also fitted with larger diameter wheels. The next two prototype aircraft were modified in the same way and delivered to Eglin Field for evaluation by the USAAF.

Four months earlier, the USAAF had placed an order for 2,500 P-51Ds (NA-109) powered by a Packard-Merlin engine, armed with six 0.5in machine guns, and with provision for a pair of external long-range fuel tanks or HVAR rockets.

The P-51D began to arrive in Europe in great numbers from March 1944 onwards; the first unit to receive the type was the 55th FG, which replaced the P-38. By D-Day, both the 8th and 9th Air Forces were well-equipped with the P-51D and the great range of the fighter was appreciated by bomber crews, who now had the company of 'little friends' to most targets in Europe. By the end of World War Two, many P-51D pilots accumulated large numbers of kills to their credit. The 357th FG alone racked up 609 aerial victories and 106 ground kills between February 1944 and April 1945.

For the RAF, the P-51D or Mustang IV, was not received with the same enthusiasm because the Mustang III was its preferred mount and the new model did not enter service until September 1944.

Post-war, the P/F-51D continued to serve the USAAF/USAF in great numbers and the type became the F-51D from 1948 onwards. The fighter was to be the backbone of the reformed Air National Guard from 1946 onwards and, by late 1948, more than 700 were on strength. The F-51D was back in action over Korea and the type proved to be much more suited to operating from rough and ready airstrips, unlike its jet-powered colleagues. One unit, the 18th FBW, actually gave up its F-80 jets in favour of the Mustang and, by the end of the conflict, the type had flown 62,607 tactical support missions for the loss of 351 aircraft.

In 1957, the last D-model, 44-74936, was withdrawn from service with the West Virginia Air National Guard.

P-51D MUSTANG

ENGINE: One 1,695hp Packard Merlin V-1650-7 12-cylinder Vee liquid-cooled
WINGSPAN: 37ft ¼in
LENGTH: 32ft 3in
HEIGHT: 8ft 8in
WING AREA: 233 sq/ft
MAX LOADED WEIGHT: 10,100lb
MAX SPEED: 437mph at 25,000ft

P-51B-1-N Mustang 43-12102, during testing of the bubble canopy installation.

Djigooblie II, a P-51D-5-NA serialled 44-13315 from 334th FS, 4th FG, undergoes maintenance at Debden. The aircraft was flown by Lt Warren H. 'Willie' Williams at the time and, after surviving the war, was sold to the Swiss Air Force in 1948 and re-serialled as J-2117.

P-51D PRODUCTION

A total of 9,703 P-51Ds were delivered to the USAAF as the NA-106, -109, -111, -122 and -124. The RAF took delivery of 282 Mustang IVs under Lend-Lease and 100 kit-form P-51Ds (NA-110) were delivered to Australia as production prototypes. Eighty of the Australian batch were assembled by CAC as CA-17s, 20 were kept back for spares and a further 120 were built as CA-18s. Also built were 1,500 P-51Ks (NA-111s), fitted with un-cuffed Aeroproducts propellers.

A fine collection of fighters at Bottisham in 1945 from the bottom: P-51D 44-14337 *"Gentle Annie"* of the 79th FS, 20th FG, flown by Col Harold J. Rau; P-51D 44-14111 *Straw Boss 2* of the 328th FS, 352nd FG, flown by Lt Col James D. Mayden; P-47D 42-26641 of the 62nd FS, 56th FG, flown by Lt Col David C. Schilling; P-51D 44-14291 *Da' Quake* flown by Lt Col John L. 'Earthquake' McGinn; and P-47D 42-26415 *Judy* of the 360th FS, 356th FG, flown by Col Philip E. Tukey, Jr.

P-51D, K and Mustang IV

A total of 282 Mustang IVs were delivered to the RAF, the first of them not entering operational service until September 1944. This aircraft, TK589, only served with the A&AEE out of Boscombe Down and is pictured on 20 August 1944.

P-51D, K and Mustang IV

Maurice Hammond's pristine North American P-51D-5-NA Mustang, 44-13521 *Marinell*. (Jarrod Cotter)

SUPERMARINE SPITFIRE

The Supermarine Spitfire began as a private venture replacing an earlier unsuccessful design to Specification F.7/30, and emerged to fill a new one, F.37/34, with the prototype flying on 5 March 1936.

An initial production order covered 310 for completion by March 1939, and production began in 1937. The first unit to be equipped was No 19 Squadron, Duxford, in August 1938, a big step up from its Gloster Gauntlets.

By the outbreak of World War Two, nine full squadrons had been equipped, and Spitfires of No 602 Squadron claimed the first victories of the war on 16 October 1939, destroying two Ju 88s and a He 111. Further large orders were placed as the type was developed, and its role in the Battle of Britain alongside the Hurricane is history. Various marks emerged and a total of 20,351 were built for the RAF, while the RN received Seafires, some which were converted from Spitfires and others new-build. Various marks of Spitfire served with 111 squadrons during World War Two, some continuing post-war.

Spitfire VBs of No 243 Squadron, Ouston, in 1942. Nearest is EN821, which later passed to No 65 Squadron before going to the RN in February 1944. It is interesting to note the other two aircraft have very small serial presentations.

Supermarine Spitfire

The Spitfire prototype, K5054, had an original pale blue overall scheme.

K5054 in a night scene after being camouflaged.

Early Spitfire production at the Vickers Supermarine factory, Eastleigh, Southampton, with Rolls-Royce Merlin engines in the foreground.

Supermarine Spitfire

Soon after D-Day, some enterprising units carried beer to Normandy, either in kegs beneath the wings of Spitfires or, as in this case, transferring the 'joy juice' to a converted (and hopefully fully cleaned out) long-range tank. A Norwegian pilot watches from the wing while RAF mess steward LAC W. Hoskins turns on the tap.

A Spitfire IXB of No 126 Squadron being rearmed and serviced in December 1944, the month in which the squadron moved from Bradwell Way to Bentwaters and began to re-equip with Mustang IIIs.

A pair of Spitfire IXEs of No 443 Squadron RCAF in March 1945 when it was based in Belgium; the lead aircraft has clipped wings of the LF.IX. No 443 was one of the first fighter squadrons to be based in Normandy after D-Day.

Supermarine Spitfire

Right: An undercarriage retraction test on an early but rather worn-looking Spitfire.

Below: Pilots of No 19 Squadron, Duxford, the first to receive Spitfires, sprint to their early aircraft in a practice scramble. Note the two-bladed fixed-pitch propellers and flat-sided canopies compared with the Mk VIII.

Spitfire FR.XIV NH927 at No 322 MU, Chakeri, Cawnpore, India, during 1947, where it and many others were flown to be scrapped.

SUPERMARINE SPITFIRE I
ENGINE: One 1,030hp Rolls-Royce Merlin II
WINGSPAN: 36ft 10in
LENGTH: 29ft 11in
HEIGHT: 11ft 5in
LOADED WEIGHT: 5,782lb
MAX SPEED: 364mph

Supermarine Spitfire

A Spitfire VIII of 92 Squadron in summer 1943 being serviced in the sunshine at Taranto, with what appears to be a damaged airship shed in the background.

Spitfire VCs of No 154 Squadron at Djedjelli, Algeria, showing their desert camouflage and tropical filters beneath the noses of the two facing aircraft. While the fate of the nearest, ES187, is not known, ES191 later went to the SAAF.

HAWKER TEMPEST

The Hawker Tempest was a logical development of the Typhoon, replacing the latter's thick wing, originally designed to house six cannon, with a new elliptical wing and, after early trials, a larger curved fin and rudder and a 2,200hp Napier Sabre engine. The prototype, HM595, flew on 2 September 1942, achieving 430mph at 20,300ft a month later, while the second aircraft, HM599, later reached 472mph but did not have the deep chin radiator and could not provide reliability.

The first production Tempest V was JN329, and first deliveries went to No 486 (New Zealand) Squadron at Beaulieu in January 1944, then to No 3 Squadron, Manston, while these and No 56 formed a Tempest Wing commanded by Wg Cdr R. P. Beamont at Newchurch to counter V1 flying bombs. They destroyed 638 and were involved in offensive sweeps over the Continent, eventually claiming some 20 Me 262 jets.

The Tempest II, with a 2,520hp Bristol Centaurus engine, was just being delivered when the Pacific War ended in September 1945. However, 452 were built and served with ten squadrons, while the Tempest V and VI, the latter a tropicalised development, served with 17, the last operational aircraft being replaced by Vampires from 1950.

A trio of Tempest Vs of No 501 Squadron at Bradwell Bay in 1944, shortly after they had replaced Spitfire XVIs.

Work on a Tempest V Sabre engine, checking the long-range tank attachments and cleaning the windscreen.

Armourers loading a No 501 Squadron Tempest V with belts of Hispano 20mm cannon ammunition.

Hawker Tempest

HAWKER TEMPEST
ENGINE: One 2,400hp Napier Sabre IIB
WINGSPAN: 41ft 0in
LENGTH: 33ft 8in
HEIGHT: 16ft 1in
LOADED WEIGHT: 12,820lb
MAX SPEED: 442mph

A batch of Tempest Vs on the Hawker production line, a few of the 201 serialled between SN102 and '355 delivered between April and October 1945.

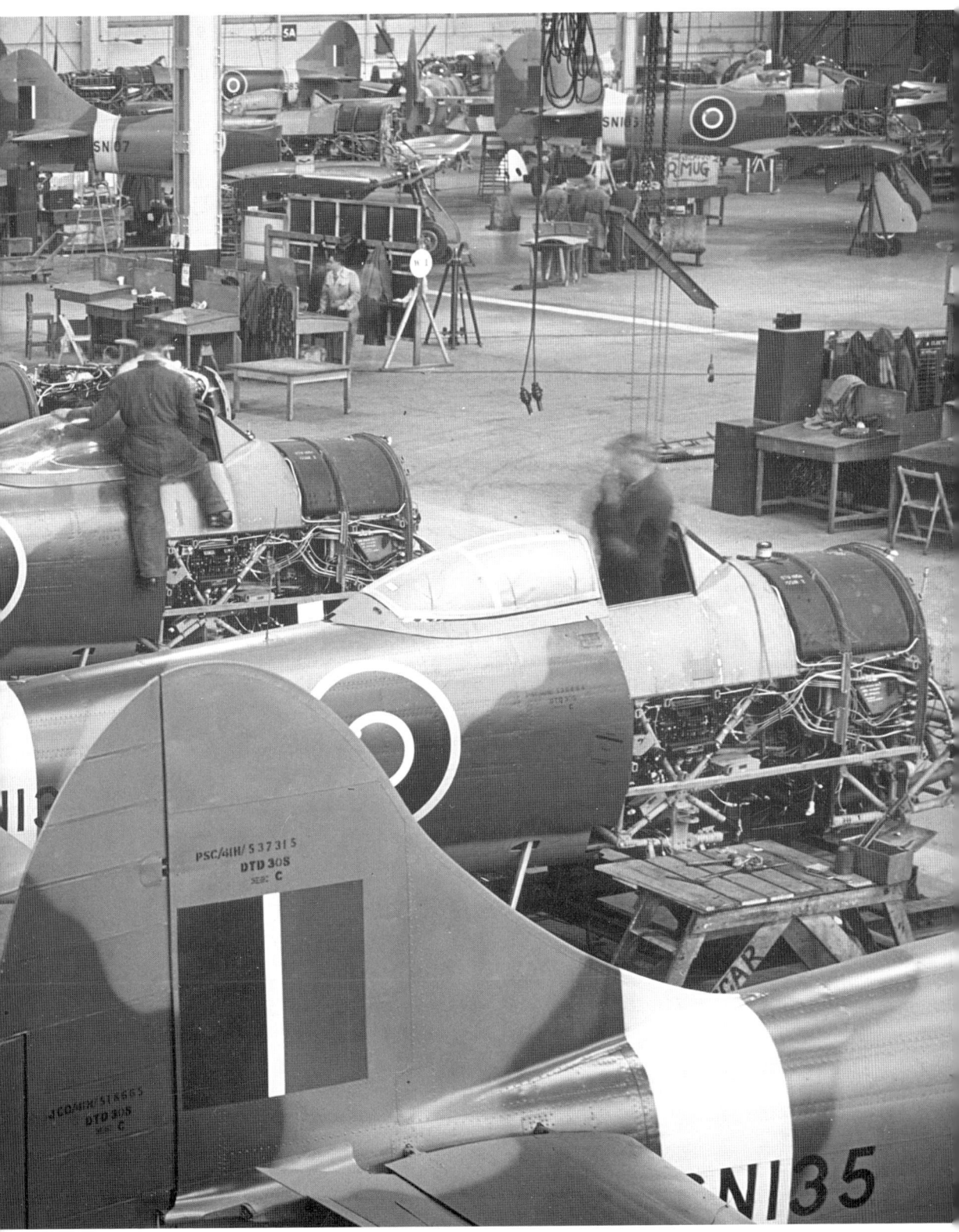

REPUBLIC P-47B AND C THUNDERBOLT

Designed by Alex Kartveli, the P-47 was built in greater numbers than any other fighter in the US aviation industry. It was a huge machine at the time and, in RAF hands, pilots would joke that they could escape the enemy's fire by running around the cockpit! In USAAF hands, the fighter served in all theatres and, in Europe especially, it was the affectionately named 'Jug', and really ground the Luftwaffe down before the Mustangs began to steel all the glory from mid-1944 onwards.

The P-47 story began in June 1940 when Kartveli submitted a radical proposal for a large, heavily armed fighter powered by the complex Pratt & Whitney R-2800 Double Wasp engine, in response to combat reports being received from Europe. It would be the 18-cylinder radial engine that dictated the design of the aircraft from the outset, the actual shape of the P-47 would just have to toe the line! A mass of pipes and ducts and a multiple exhaust system that led to the rear fuselage, resulted in an aircraft with a very deep fuselage that extended below the wing. This was not an ideal situation for the designer who was well aware that the R-2800 would need a big, 12ft 2in diameter propeller, and the resulting undercarriage that was needed to provide sufficient ground clearance would have to be very long. The problem of a long undercarriage that was strong enough to overcome operational use was solved by designing a main gear which shortened by nine inches as it retracted. This still gave plenty of room in the wing outboard of the wheel wells for four 0.5in machine guns and their ammunition boxes, which extended almost to the end of the wing. All fuel tanks, which were self-sealing, were positioned in the fuselage below and slightly forward of the cockpit. The spacious cockpit was air-conditioned and was furnished with a wide range of controls for systems that were not normally seen in a fighter. The canopy, which was fronted by a deep Vee windscreen, was upward hinged in the early aircraft

A pair of P-47Cs of the 61st FS, 56th FG, operating out of King's Cliffe in early 1943 during the unit's working up period. 41-6352 went missing on 31 October 1944, while 41-6267 was later transferred to the 552nd FTS, 495th FTG, and crashed at Bricklin Farm near Whitchurch on 28 September 1944.

and, behind a sharp upper line, gave the fighter the early nickname 'razorback'.

The unpainted prototype was first flown by Lowry L. Brabham from Farmingdale Field on 6 May 1941, a mere eight months after it was ordered. Such a complex aircraft inevitably produced a complex array of problems but all involved could still see the potential in this big fighter and, despite misgivings, the USAAC ordered 171 P-47Bs and this was followed by an order for 602 improved models, the P-47C. The first production P-47B was delivered in March 1942, complete with a sliding canopy, metal-skinned control services and an R-2800-21 engine.

The first unit to receive the P-47B was the 56th FG in May 1942, a unit which was destined to operate the Thunderbolt until mid-1945. The 56th FG was shipping across the Atlantic to join the 8th Air Force in England in January 1943 where it would operate the P-47C. The 'B' was used solely for flying training and flight testing. The 'C' was a foot longer than the 'B', could carry a single 500lb bomb or a 200-US gallon drop tank, a useful feature if the Thunderbolt was going to make a name for itself as a long-range escort.

The 4th FG was already established in England and later the 78th FG also re-equipped with the P-47C, but it was the former unit which took the type into combat for the first time. The P-47 made its operational debut on 10 March 1943, when 14 P-47Cs of the 334th FS, 4th FG, carried out Rodeo 179, a sweep of the French and Belgian coastline. The first major clash with the enemy did not come until 15 April when the 4th FG met Fw 190s of JG2 and JG26, which resulted in a single kill for the American group and the first for the P-47 by Maj Don Blakeslee. The P-47C broke the ice in combat for the USAAF and many remained in service into late 1944 when it was already time to make way for the next generation of Thunderbolt that was pouring out of the factories.

Republic P-47B and C Thunderbolt

Half a dozen early production P-47Bs of the 61st FS, 56th FG, in the US in September 1942, not long after the group was taken over by Col Hubert A. Zemke. This is a black and white still from a colour film and Zemke's aircraft, closest to the camera, displays blue, orange and red bands on the rear fuselage and around the forward engine cowling, which denotes all three of the group's squadron colours.

REPUBLIC P-47C

FIRST FLIGHT: (XP-47B) 6 May 1941

ENGINE: One 2,000hp (2,300hp WEP) Pratt & Whitney R-2800-21 engine

WINGSPAN: 40ft 9 5/16in

LENGTH: 36ft 1 3/16in

MAX SPEED: 433mph at 30,000ft

INITIAL CLIMB RATE: 2,780ft/min

ARMAMENT: Eight .50in Browning machine guns and one 500lb bomb or 200 US-gallon fuel tank

Six P-47Cs of the 62nd FS, commanded by Maj David Schilling, captured during a training sortie out of Horsham St Faith in mid-1943.

A P-47C of the 78th FG out of Duxford keeps a close eye on its charge, which, on this occasion, is a 91st BG B-17 from neighbouring Bassingbourn. The 78th FG operated the P-47 into 1944 when it re-equipped with the P-51.

REPUBLIC P-47D THUNDERBOLT

By far the most prolific variant of the Thunderbolt family was the 'D' model, of which 12,602 were built out of a total production of 15,660 aircraft. The P-47D, which was first ordered on 13 October 1941, several weeks before the US entered World War Two, did not reach operational service until mid-1943. The P-47D should really have been spread over several variants because it encompassed a vast range of modifications, including an ever-improving engine with water injection and emergency combat boost, a modified supercharger, better pilot armour and multi-ply tyres that could stand the punishment of rough strips under full loads.

From the beginning of production to the very end in 1945, the P-47D changed in appearance and improved in performance. The very first machines built (approximately 110) at Farmingdale, Long Island, were actually identical to P-47Cs but, from the P-47D-1 to D-6, D-10 and D-11 blocks that modifications unique to the 'D' model began to be incorporated. From block D-20 onwards, the capability of the Thunderbolt was further improved with the introduction of a 'universal' wing with pylons for 1,000lb bombs or 150 US-gallon drop tanks, plus a similar load on the centreline. This gave the P-47D the capability to escort the 8th Air Force all the way to Berlin and back if necessary with enough fuel to strafe targets of opportunity on the way home. It was in the latter role that the Thunderbolt built up a formidable reputation, especially during the final 12 months of the war in Europe,

as an excellent ground attack aircraft, making full use of the brutal firepower of its eight 0.5 machine guns.

One problem that had been plaguing all Allied fighter aircraft up to 1943 was that of visibility to the rear. All fighters had, on average, a 20° blind spot which was partly cured by the introduction of the British Malcolm hood that worked well in the Spitfire, the P-51B/C and in part with the P-47 as well. When the British produced a bubble canopy for the Typhoon, the idea quickly caught on and the Americans soon adopted it for its two main fighters, the P-47 and the P-51. In July 1943, a single P-47D was modified with a chopped down rear fuselage and clear-view bubble canopy designed for the Typhoon. The aircraft was designated the XP-47K and the hood was so popular that it was introduced into the Farmingdale production line from the P-47D-25-RE and at the Evansville factory from the P-47D-26-RA. Subsequently, from block 25 onwards, Farmingdale would produce 2,547 'bubble-top' P-47s and Evansville 4,632.

By early 1944, virtually all P-47s were delivered in a natural finish, which further increased the performance – even the gross weight had increased to 17,500lb. This was counteracted by more powerful engines, combined with a four-blade paddle-type propeller that also helped to improve the climb rate. Chopping down the rear fuselage had caused some directional stability problems but this was partly cured with the addition of a shallow dorsal spin that stretched from the front of the fin to the rear of the canopy. From block 35 onwards, the P-47D was also fitted with ten zero-length attachments for 5in HVAR and a K-14 computing gunsight giving the Thunderbolt even more clout in the ground attack role.

Republic P-47D-28-RE 44-19566 of the 82nd FS, 78th FG, pictured at Duxford. Nicknamed 'The Duxford Eagles', the unit moved to its Cambridgeshire home from Goxhill in north Lincolnshire in April 1943 and remained there until October 1945. The unit re-equipped with the P-51D in December 1944 but returned to the P-47 while operating from Straubing in Germany during the post-war occupation period.

Republic P-47D Thunderbolt

While the P-51 replaced the P-47 in the long-range escort role, the Thunderbolt still ended the war with 3,752 aerial kills to its credit in more 746,000 sorties. During the early months of 1944, the P-47 shot down 570 out of 873 enemy aircraft claimed and, from January to June, maintained the rate by claiming 900 out of 1,983 kills. In Europe alone, the P-47 flew 423,435 sorties, which was more than all of the P-51s, P-38s and P-40s combined. By the end of the war, only the 56th FG was still flying the P-47 (by choice) claiming 677.5 aerial victories and 311 aircraft destroyed on the ground for the loss of 128 Thunderbolts. Out of this group, the lead pilot was Lt Col Francis S. 'Gabby' Gabreski, with 31 victories to his name followed by Maj Robert S. Johnson with 27 and Col David C. Schilling with 22.5; 40 56th FG pilots achieved 'ace' status. In the fighter-bomber role, the P-47 claimed 86,000 pieces to railway rolling stock, 9,000 locomotives, 6,000 military vehicles and 68,000 lorries destroyed. All of this equates to a service record that was second to none.

REPUBLIC P-47D-25-RE

FIRST FLIGHT: December 1942
ENGINE: One 2,535hp Pratt & Whitney R-2800-59W Double Wasp engine
WINGSPAN: 40ft 9¼in
LENGTH: 36ft 1¾in
MAX SPEED: 433mph
ARMAMENT: Eight .50in Browning machine guns and external load of up to 2,500lb

Main: P-47D-11-RE 42-75329 *Miss Second Front* of the 395th FS ('A7'), 368th FG. The 9th AF receives some maintenance at A-3 (Cardonville) in Normandy in August 1944. Under the command of Col Gilbert L. Meyers at the time, the 368th FG gave support to Allied troops from D-Day plus one.

Right: 1st Lt Donald J. Corrigan chats to his crew chief while sitting on the wing of P-47D-22-RE 25-25771 of the 352nd FS, 353rd FG, at Raydon. This particular aircraft was paid for with War Bonds purchased by the employees of the Republic Aviation Corporation. The big fighter was lost on 10 June 1944, during a dive-bombing mission against the enemy-held airfield at Renne; the pilot, 2nd Lt Virgil C. Johnson, was killed.

Republic P-47D Thunderbolt

LATER P-47 VARIANTS

(P-47D) major production model, 2,300hp R-2800-21W or 2,535hp R-2800-59W with water-injection, large number of modifications in various blocks, 12,602 built; (XP-47E) one example with pressurised cockpit; (XP-47F) one experimental example with laminar-flow wings; (P-47G) razor-back model built by Curtiss-Wright, 354 built; (XP-47H) development of P-47D with 2,300hp Chrysler XIV-2200-1 liquid-cooled 16-cylinder inverted-Vee, length 39ft 2in and maximum speed 490mph; (XP-47J) based on P-47D with lightened structure and 2,800hp R-2800-57(C) radial with a CH-5 turbocharger, six 0.5in machine guns, first flown November 1943 and in August 1944 reached 504mph; (XP-47K) clearview teardrop hood from a Typhoon, first flown 3 July 1943, one built; (P-47M) based on a P-47D with 2,800hp R-2800-57(C) and CH-5 turbocharger, first flown mid-1944, sometimes fitted with six 0.5in machine guns, max speed 470mph, 133 built including three prototypes; (P-47N) long-range model for the Pacific fitted with new wing tanks, broad ailerons and square cut tips, stronger undercarriage, 2,800hp R-2800-57(C), max speed 460mph, 1,816 built.

Main: A pair of 350th FG, 12th AF, P-47Ds on patrol close to the Austrian border on 25 February 1945. Nearest to the camera is P-47D-30-RE 44-20978 *Torrid Tess*, being flown by 1st Lt Homer J. St Onge. *Torrid Tess* was shot down during a strafing mission in the Po Valley on 27 April 1945, forcing St Onge to bale out. He managed to evade capture with the help of partisans.

CURTISS P-40, A TO C/TOMAHAWK MK I, IIA AND IIB

There was no doubting that the P-63/Hawk 75 made quite an impression when it first appeared, but it was not destined to serve the USAAC in great numbers. There may have been some expectation that the next Curtiss fighter to be designed by Donovan Berlin's team would be even more impressive but, sadly for the USAAC and future USAAF at least, this was not to be.

Rather than going back to drawing board, Berlin produced the P-40, which was little more than a development of the P-36 rather than another 'state-of-the-art' fighter. Clearly, Curtiss was protecting, to some degree, the investment of time and money that it had already put into the P-36 and presumed that,

with little effort, the P-40 would be noticeably better. However, the result was only modest improvement in performance, a distinct lack of agility and from the mouths of those men who had to fight in them, a distinctive disadvantage against all of the main adversaries. On the plus side, the P-40 retained the P-36's pleasant handling characteristics, was one of the most robust single-seat fighters of the entire war and was available in great numbers at a reasonable price.

The prototype, XP-40, which was the 10th production P-36 of the line, was first flown by test pilot Edward Elliot on 14 October 1938. Powered by an Allison V-1710 liquid-cooled engine, the aircraft was given the Curtiss designation Hawk

81A. Despite early misgivings, which mainly revolved around the aircraft's disappointing performance, an order for 524 aircraft was placed by the USAAC on 27 April 1939, the first of which flew on 4 April 1940. The first 200 of the early P-40s were only armed with a pair of .30in machines guns in the wings and were delivered without armour, bullet-proof windscreens or self-sealing fuel tanks. These were all features that would evolve and improve with combat experience and be rectified from the 200th production aircraft onwards, which became the P-40B. The main feature that differed between the P-40 and the P-40B was the addition of a pair of .30in machine guns in the wings. In total, 131 P-40Bs were built and the remainder of the initial 524 aircraft order was rounded off with 193 P-40Cs, which featured self-sealing fuels tanks and the ability to carry an external drop tank on the centreline.

Like the Hawk 75 before it, a large order for 230 P-40s was placed by France, but delivery could not take place because the country fell in June 1940. Like the Hawk, the order, which would expand to 1,180 aircraft including the French machines, was taken over by the RAF, which christened the aircraft the Tomahawk (Model 81). The RAF Tomahawks were spread over three different marks: the Mk I being the same as a P-40 but with four wing guns; the Mk IIA, which was the same as a P-40B: and the Mk IIB, which was the equivalent to the P-40C. The RAF's Mk IIs had US radio equipment and six .303in machine guns and saw service with 2, 26, 73, 112, 136, 168, 239, 241, 250, 403, 414, 430 and 616 Squadrons. The type also saw service with 3 (RAAF) Squadron and 2 and 4 (SAAF) Squadrons.

One hundred aircraft from the RAF's order were diverted to China, where 90 of them gave excellent service with the American Volunteer Group (AVG) 'Flying Tigers'. Under the AVG's leader Claire Chennault, the P-40 pilots were trained to get the best out of an aircraft that was inferior to the enemy but, despite this, 115 enemy aircraft were brought down over a six and half month period for the loss of just four P-40s.

There were 635 Tomahawk IIBs (P-40C) delivered to the RAF, including AK431 which first served with 5 (SAAF) Squadron and finally 73 OTU at Abu Sueir, Egpyt, where it is pictured in May 1943. A Hurricane fighter-bomber training unit, this aircraft remained on 73 OTU strength until 29 June 1944.

Curtiss P-40, A to C/Tomahawk Mk I, IIA and IIB

Above and right: P-40s (Model 81) pour out of the Curtiss plant at Buffalo, New York, in 1940 in response to the USAAC's initial production order of 524 aircraft ordered on 26 April 1939. Two hundred P-40s were actually built, serialled 39-156–289 (134) and 40-292–357 (66).

CURTISS P-40B
FIRST FLIGHT: (XP-40) 14 October 1938
ENGINE: One 1,090hp Allison V-1710-33
WINGSPAN: 37ft 3½in
LENGTH: 31ft 8¾in
MAX SPEED: 351mph at 15,000ft
ARMAMENT: Two .50in and four .30in Colt-Browning machine guns

Below: One of a batch of 471 Tomahawk IIBs delivered to the RAF by Curtiss between December 1940 and October 1941 under Contract A-84, AK186 is pictured in service with 414 (Sarnia Imperials) Squadron. Formed at Croydon on 12 August 1941, in the Army Co-operation role, the unit operated the Tomahawk, along with the Lysander Mk III, until it was replaced by the Mustang in June 1942.

Hawker Typhoon

The second production Typhoon, R7577, served only with the makers and the A&AEE, Boscombe Down, before being struck off charge on 2 December 1943.

Six of No 56 Squadron's early Typhoons, the squadron operated the type from September 1941 to May 1944. Note the white recognition band from the inboard cannon.

HAWKER TYPHOON

The Hawker Typhoon was designed to Specification F.18/37 as a high-performance interceptor but its early days were dogged with problems affecting the big Napier Sabre engine.

Two prototypes were ordered, plus two similar Tornadoes (see details at the end of this book), and the first prototype Typhoon, P2512, flew on 24 February 1940. It was badly damaged in May, and the second, P5216, did not fly until May 1941, since Hawker was busy with Hurricane production.

While 15 development Typhoons were built by Hawker at Langley, an initial 500 production aircraft were built by Gloster, which flew its first on 27 May 1941. The first operational aircraft went to 56 Squadron, Duxford, and suffered many problems, but the Typhoon came into its own as a ground attack aircraft and eventually equipped 30 squadrons. Total Gloster production reached 3,315. It was the RAF's first 400mph fighter and was replaced by the Tempest from 1945.

Hawker Typhoon

More early Typhoons with what appears to be the whole of No 181 Squadron wanting to be in the picture.

A Typhoon waits to be bombed-up, the bomb racks just visible beneath the inboard cannon.

Typhoon EK266 of No 182 Squadron displays the unique recognition markings of four black and three white stripes, adopted to distinguish it from the Fw 190, which, to the anti-aircraft gunners, it resembled. They should not be confused with the 'invasion stripes' worn from D-Day – three white and two black.

Hawker Typhoon

HAWKER TYPHOON IB
ENGINE: One 2,200hp Napier Sabre
WINGSPAN: 41ft 7in
LENGTH: 31ft 11in
HEIGHT: 15ft 3in
LOADED WEIGHT: 13,250lb
MAX SPEED: 412mph

Engine fitters at work on the Napier Sabre engine of Typhoon R8220 of No 56 Squadron. Early Typhoons had the 'car door' type entry to the cockpit.

Westland Whirlwind

Whirlwind prototype L6844 flew in October 1938. During its life, it was flown by the Royal Aircraft Establishment (RAE), the A&AEE and the Air Fighting Development Unit (AFDU) before becoming maintenance airframe 3063M in March 1941.

WESTLAND WHIRLWIND

The Westland Whirlwind was the RAF's first single-seat twin-engine fighter, and two prototypes, L6844 and L6845, were ordered, the first flying on 11 October 1938. Although 340 had been ordered, production was limited to 114, with brief trials at Martlesham Heath and Northolt being undertaken by P6966 and P6967 in June 1940.

The Whirlwind was the only user of the Rolls-Royce Peregrine engine, which was to prove troublesome, but in early tests, the Whirlwind was faster than the Spitfire below 10,000ft, had an excellent field of view and a heavy armament of four 20mm Hispano cannon. Although originally intended as a day and night fighter, the latter role had been adopted by the radar-equipped Blenheim 1F, which required a two-man crew, so the Whirlwind was confined to daylight operations. The first began in December 1940 with No 263 Squadron, Exeter, while offensive sweeps followed in June 1941, and the only other Whirlwind squadron, No 137, was formed in September 1941 at Charmy Down. Shortly after, modifications were made to adopt the fighter-bomber role, with underwing provision for two 250lb or 500lb bombs and in this role the aircraft was very successful in offensive sweeps across the Channel.

In June 1943, No 137 Squadron re-equipped with Hurricane IVs, No 263 Squadron following with Typhoons in December that year.

P6967 was the second of two pre-production aircraft and had small intakes above the engines not fitted on succeeding aircraft.

ALLIED FIGHTERS OF WORLD WAR TWO: US AND BRITAIN 163

Westland Whirlwind

WESTLAND WHIRLWIND
ENGINES: Two 885hp Rolls-Royce Peregrine
WINGSPAN: 45ft 0in
LENGTH: 32ft 9in
HEIGHT: 11ft 7in
LOADED WEIGHT: 19,356lb
MAX SPEED: 360mph

A Whirlwind of No 137 Squadron about to receive its bomb load, with delivery made easier by the use of an industrial Standard Fordson Tractor.

Westland Whirlwind

Armourers loading the 20mm cannon ammunition boxes, an easy job with the removable nose cover.

Although initially delivered to No 137 Squadron, Whirlwind P7062 later went to No 263 in whose marks it is seen. It was lost during a practice attack when it hit trees and spun into the ground near Wroughton on 19 February 1943.

P7110, the 102nd Whirlwind built, seen prior to delivery to No 263 Squadron, which unfortunately lost it when an engine cut on approach to Warmwell on 13 July 1943.

WAITING IN THE WINGS – BRITISH

This final section illustrates a selection of aircraft that were under development during World War Two, but which, for various reasons explained here, did not achieve quantity production or make it to active service during the war.

BOULTON PAUL P.92/2: Boulton Paul was building the Defiant prototype in 1936 with its turret containing four 0.303 machine guns when Specification F.18/36 was issued for a twin-engine three-seat fighter with a four-cannon turret to deal with the all-metal bombers being built.

The Air Ministry subsequently amended the requirement to Specification F.11/37 and invited tenders which stipulated an excellent view, a speed of 370mph at 35,000ft, ability to maintain height on one engine and a design that would permit quick build at dispersed sites. Boulton Paul tendered against Armstrong Whitworth, Bristol, Hawker, Short and Supermarine, winning an order for three prototypes, two with Rolls-Royce Vulture engines and one with Napier Sabres.

Work began on the first two in mid-1937, and to examine dynamics, a half-scale wooden flying model (the P.92/2) with 130hp engines was built by Heston Aircraft, but in May 1940, the P.92 was cancelled. Nevertheless, Boulton Paul decided to complete the P.92/2, V3142, which flew at Heston in spring 1941 but after testing the aircraft was broken up.

HAWKER TORNADO:

Developed alongside the Typhoon, the Tornado was Vulture-powered but had a similar airframe to the Typhoon, and the prototype, P5219, flew on 6 October 1939, with a second, P5224, following in December 1940. An order for 200, to be built by Avro, was placed and the first, R7936, flew in August 1941, later being used as a test-bed for various propellers.

Continuing problems with the Vulture and Rolls-Royce's heavy involvement with Merlin production led to the cancellation of the Avro contract but one more Tornado, HG641, was assembled by Hawker at Langley with a Bristol Centaurus radial engine and flew on 23 October 1941. Although no orders followed, it proved to be a useful introduction for the engine later used in the Tempest II.

WESTLAND WELKIN: Originally designed to Specification F.4/40, later amended to F.7/41, for a two-seat high-altitude fighter, Welkin prototype DG558/G flew on 1 November 1942, with the second, DG562/G, following in March 1943. Despite problems with the engines causing forced-landings, an order was placed for 100, with a further 100 to follow. During tests at the A&AEE, there were a number of accidents including engine problems and propeller failures, and with the expected German high-altitude bomber threat failing to materialise, the need for the Welkin disappeared. Although 75 production aircraft plus 25 airframes were built, none were delivered to the RAF and were stored for eventual breaking-up. Though a few Welkin Is were removed from store and trialled by some units. The requirement for a two-seat night fighter led to DX386 being taken out of store and converted into Welkin NF.II PF370, which flew on 23 October 1944, but it had a poor performance and no more were built.

GLOSTER F.9/37: Failing to attract much attention in spite of its performance, Gloster's twin-engine fighter to Specification F.9/37 drew on an earlier Folland design that had been dropped when the Defiant was ordered. The new aircraft was a single-seater of metal stressed-skin construction with fabric-covered control surfaces and the prototype, L7999, with Taurus engines, flew on 3 April 1939, with two 20mm cannon in the nose, although six had been specified. Favourable comments had been made at the A&AEE where it had reached 360mph, the highest speed reached by a British military aircraft, but following an accident it was re-engined with 900hp Taurus engines, reducing its speed by 28mph. The second prototype, L8002, flew on 22 February 1940, with two 885hp Rolls-Royce Peregrine engines (as used in the Whirlwind), but production orders were placed for the Beaufighter.

Waiting in the Wings – British

SUPERMARINE SPITEFUL: In an effort to increase speeds at which an aircraft could be flown, a series of high-speed aerofoil sections were needed, and Supermarine, in collaboration with the National Physical Laboratory, designed a new laminar flow wing for an aircraft designed to Specification F.1/43, which emerged as the Spiteful, and 21 were ordered. The prototype, NN660, was a Spitfire XIV fitted with a laminar flow wing and flew on 30 June 1944, but was lost two weeks later. The second, NN664, also flew on 30 June 1944, but exhibited handling and stability problems. Delays in incorporating modifications to production aircraft and the approach of jets led to production being cut to 17, and the first production Spiteful was RB515, flown in April 1945. The single Mk XVI, RB518, achieved a speed of 494mph, but no Spitefuls entered RAF service, although 16 of a naval version, the Seafang, were built and undertook trials. However, by then the RN was committed to its first jet, the Supermarine Attacker, which ironically used a version of the Spiteful and Seafang's laminar flow wing!

VICKERS 432: Intended to meet Specification F.7/41 for a high-altitude fighter, the Vickers 432's design was helped by the company's experience with the high-altitude Wellington V, which incorporated a pressure cabin. The 432 was to have six 20mm Hispano cannon mounted in a large ventral fairing, but these were not fitted in the only prototype, DZ217, which flew at Farnborough on 24 December 1942. Handling problems and failure of satisfactory engine operation above 23,000ft resulted in cancellation of the programme at the end of 1943, by which time threats of German high-altitude bombing had gone.

MARTIN BAKER M.B.5: The Martin-Baker company had flown its M.B.3 fighter built to Specification F.18/39 in 1942 but had lost it in a take-off crash in September that year. Undeterred, the company built a much improved version, the M.B.5, to the same specification but with a much larger engine driving contra-rotating propellers (originally de Havilland, later Rotol). The first flight of the only M.B.5, R2496, was at Harwell on 23 May 1944, and it was soon obvious that it was an outstanding design with excellent performance and had ease of accessibility to the cockpit with its sliding one-piece canopy.

Plans in 1945 to attack the world's speed record with the engine de-rated to 2,480hp recorded a speed of 484mph on a course near Gloucester. Unfortunately, this came to nothing, for the day of the jet had arrived and so no production orders were received.

MILES M.20/2: With production of the Hurricane and Spitfire going ahead in 1938, there were fears that rates could not be stepped up in time to fully equip the RAF if a European war materialised. The Miles company, builders of a range of light aircraft and the RAF's first monoplane trainer, the Master I, submitted the design of a wooden fighter with a fixed, spatted undercarriage, originally to be powered by a Rolls-Royce Peregrine engine, but as these were in demand for the Whirlwind, it was redesigned to be Merlin-powered as the M.20/2, whose thick wings carried eight 0.303 Browning machine guns and had space for a further four.

The clear view cockpit canopy provided the best view of any fighter and the prototype, AX834, flew on 15 September 1940, only 65 days after design had begun. A speed of 333mph was slightly better than the Hurricane but no orders were placed for this or a proposed naval version.

WAITING IN THE WINGS – US

SEVERSKY P-35: One of the very early stages of development that would lead to the excellent P-47 Thunderbolt, the Alexander Kartveli-designed Seversky P-35 was a single-seat fighter that entered USAAC service in 1937. Only 196 were built, the first of them serving with the 1st PG at Selfridge Field, Michigan, by which time it was already on the verge of becoming obsolete. At the beginning of World War Two, the few that were still in service with the 3rd and 17th PS were hopelessly outclassed by the Japanese fighters during the routing of the Philippines. The last surviving machine flew a strafing sortie with a P-40 against Japanese troops at Macajalar Bay on 3 May 1942. The aircraft pictured is being prepared for trials work with NACA at Langley Field in April 1939.

CURTISS XP-62: A one-off prototype, the XP-62, was designed to be a high-performance, heavily armed fighter for the USAAF. Several project reviews, which changed the specification, resulted in the XP-62 not flying until 21 July 1943, and then, after a great deal of time and expenditure, the programme was cancelled on 21 September.

FISHER XP-75 EAGLE: The XP-75 was the result of a USAAF requirement issued in September 1942 for a fighter with a very high rate of climb fitted with the most powerful liquid-cooled engine available at the time, the 2,885hp Allison V-3420. Originally contracted for just two prototypes, 13 XP-75s were eventually built, the first of them flying with a 2,600hp V-3420-19 engine on 17 November 1943. The project was plagued with technical problems and, by the time these were ironed out, the aircraft performed no better than the in-service P-38, P-47 and P-51.

BELL P-63 KINGCOBRA: This highly successful development of the P-39 Airacobra, the P-63 Kingcobra was not accepted by the USAAF simply because it was slightly inferior in performance to the P-51 Mustang and as such was not ordered into production. However, there was a desperate need for fighters in the Soviet Union and out of a total production run of 3,303 aircraft, between 2,440 and 2,680 were delivered to Russia. Several modifications were implemented under Soviet influence and the first machine was delivered in October 1943 under the caveat that the fighter should only be used on the Soviet Far Eastern Front rather than in the west against the Luftwaffe. This rule was, unsurprisingly, flouted by the Russians. Some 114 P-63s also joined the French Armée de l'Air in 1945, which was too late to see action during World War Two. The Kingcobras did see service in the First Indochina War before being retired in 1951. The fighter also saw service with the Honduran Air Force during the post-war period.

ALLIED FIGHTERS OF WORLD WAR TWO: US AND BRITAIN

Waiting in the Wings – US

BELL P-59 AIRACOMET: Despite being America's first jet fighter, the USAAF were unimpressed with the aircraft's performance and, as a result, the contract was halved and only 66 were built. Only the P-59B, of which 20 were built, entered USAAF service with the 412th FG, more for familiarisation training rather than any form of operational use. The aircraft pictured is P-59B 44-22633, which was nicknamed the 'Reluctant Robot'. It was written off at Muroc Army Air Base (now Edwards Air Force Base) in October 1948 but remains extant there to this day.

NORTHROP XP-56 BLACK BULLET: One of the most striking experimental fighters developed in the US during World War Two, the first of two prototype XP-56s first flew from Muroc on 30 September 1943. The XP-56 was the most difficult to handle of the three pusher fighters presented to the USAAF and, during a high speed taxi, the first aircraft was destroyed after a tyre blew out. The second aircraft was first flown on 23 March 1944, but only low speeds were ever attained before the programme was cancelled in 1946. The second prototype, 42-38353, is pictured on jacks at Muroc and today is preserved in the Smithsonian Institute's National Air and Space Museum in Washington DC.

VULTEE XP-54 'SWOOSE GOOSE': One of three unusual designs submitted to the USAAC in late 1940 under proposal R-40C, the XP-54 displayed a number of unique features. The aircraft's pressurised cockpit was accessed from below, the pilot's seat being part of an elevator system. Lowered electrically, the pilot sat in his seat which was then raised into the cockpit. The aircraft's long nose could be raised three degrees up from the horizontal and six degrees down. The Lycoming engine was mounted in the pusher configuration and, after the maiden flight of the first of two prototypes, performance was found to be severely lacking. The second prototype (pictured) was fitted with an experimental supercharger but only made one flight before it was resigned to become a 'hangar queen' to keep the first aircraft flying.

CURTISS-WRIGHT XP-55 ASCENDER: Another pusher design that was submitted in competition with the 'Swoose Goose', the XP-55 Ascender had a canard configuration, swept wings and twin vertical tails. Only three prototypes were built, the first flying from Scott Field in the hands of Curtiss test pilot J. Harvey Gray on 19 July 1943. The prototype was to be short-lived because Gray had to abandon the machine in an inverted spin on 13 November 1943. Like the 'Swoose Goose', the performance of the XP-55 was poor and, by 1944, with the jet-age already dawning, the programme had been cancelled.

Waiting in the Wings – US

VULTEE XP-81: The XP-81 was a promising aircraft that was designed as a long-range escort fighter, but with a contract awarded for two prototypes on 11 February 1945, the odds of the type entering service before the end of the war was always slim. The uniqueness of the aircraft was its dual power-plants, which comprised one General Electric turboprop and one turbojet. The idea was that the turboprop would provide economy while in cruise and the turbojet would give the aircraft the extra burst of speed it would need in combat. The first prototype, 44-91000, flew on 11 February 1945, but with the war drawing to a close, a pre-production order was cancelled, although development of the aircraft continued until 1947.

NORTH AMERICAN XP-82 TWIN MUSTANG: The last American piston-engine fighter to be ordered into production by the USAAF, the P-82 Twin Mustang was another design for a long-range escort which failed to see service during World War Two. However, during the post-war period, the aircraft proved to be a vital stop-gap in the Air Force's night fighter all-weather capability and was credited with scoring the first enemy kills during the opening days of the Korean War.

LOCKHEED P-80 SHOOTING STAR: One of the world's most successful first-generation jets, the P-80 was designed, built and delivered to the USAAF in just 143 days! The aircraft single-handedly brought the future USAF into the jet age and many of the 1,715 built saw extensive action during the Korean War as the F-80. The aircraft was in a different league to the early P-59 and would go on to be developed into the F-94 Starfire and the equally successful T-33 trainer. P-80B 45-8478 of the New Mexico Air National Guard, 118th Fighter-Interceptor Squadron, is pictured here.

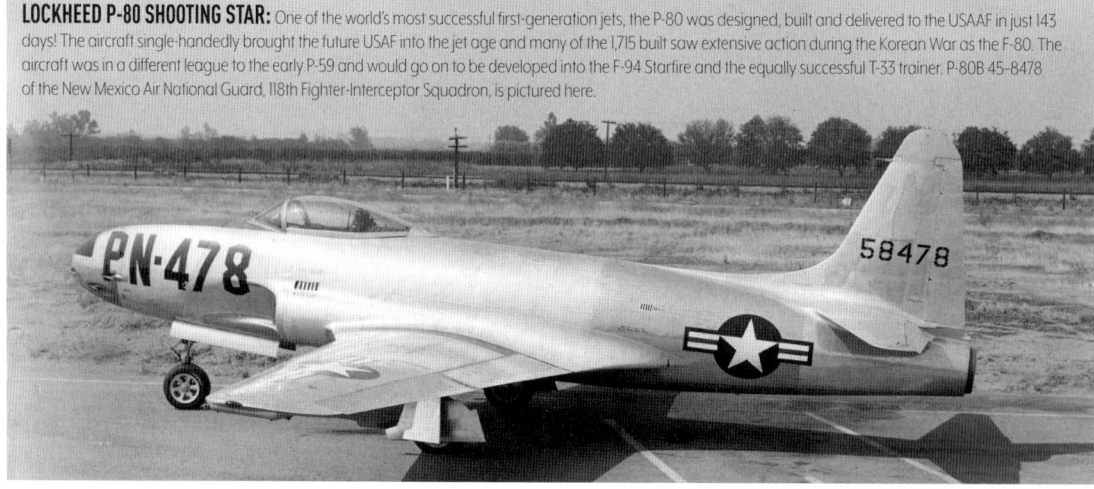